Behind the Screen

Behind the Screen

*Content Moderation in the Shadows
of Social Media*

SARAH T. ROBERTS

Yale UNIVERSITY PRESS

New Haven and London

Yale University Press books may be purchased in quantity for educational, business, or promotional use. For information, please e-mail sales.press@yale.edu (U.S. office) or sales@yaleup.co.uk (U.K. office).

Set in Minion type by IDS Infotech Ltd.
Printed in the United States of America.

ISBN 978-0-300-23588-3 (hardcover : alk. paper)
Library of Congress Control Number: 2018963972
A catalogue record for this book is available from the British Library.

This paper meets the requirements of ANSI/NISO Z39.48-1992 (Permanence of Paper).

10 9 8 7 6 5 4 3 2 1

For my grandparents
For my parents
For Patricia

" 'Human-Computer Interaction' . . . I mean, what other kind is there?"

—DR. CHRISTINE PAWLEY, 2009

Contents

Behind the Screen

Behind the Internet

This book represents the culmination of eight years of research into the work of commercial content moderation of the internet, the workers who do it, and the reasons behind why their work is both essential and, seemingly paradoxically, invisible. Commercial content moderators are professional people paid to screen content uploaded to the internet's social media sites on behalf of the firms that solicit user participation. Their job is to evaluate and adjudicate online content generated by users and decide if it can stay up or must be deleted. They act quickly, often screening thousands of images, videos, or text postings a day. And, unlike the virtual community moderators of an earlier internet and of some prominent sites today, they typically have no special or visible status to speak of within the internet platform they moderate.[1] Instead, a key to their activity is often to remain as discreet and undetectable as possible.

Content moderation of online social and information spaces is not new; people have been creating and enforcing rules of engagement in online social spaces since the inception of those spaces and throughout the past four decades. What is new, however, is the industrial-scale organized content moderation activities of professionals who are paid for their evaluative gatekeeping services, and who undertake the work they do on behalf of large-scale commercial entities: social media firms, news outlets, companies that have an online presence they would like to have managed, apps and dating tools, and so on. It is a phenomenon that has grown up at scale alongside the proliferation of social media, digital information seeking, and online connected social and other activity as a part of everyday life.

As a result of the incredible global scale, reach, and impact of mainstream social media platforms, these companies demand a workforce dispersed around the world, responding to their need for monitoring and brand protection around the clock, every single day. Once the scope of this activity became clear to me, along with the realization that talking about it would require coining a descriptive name for this work and the people who do it, I settled on the term "commercial content moderation" to reflect the new reality. I also use some other terms interchangeably to stand in for commercial content moderators, such as "moderators" or "mods," "screeners," or other, more generic terms; unless otherwise specifically noted, I am always talking about the professional people who do this work as a job and for a source of income. There are many terms to describe this type of work, and employers, as well as the moderators themselves, may use any one of them or others even more abstract.

Of course, commercial content moderators are not literally invisible; indeed, if anyone should seek them out, they will be there—in plush Silicon Valley tech headquarters, in sparse cube farms in warehouses or skyscrapers, in rural America or hyperurban Manila, working from home on a laptop in the Pacific Northwest while caring for kids—in places around the world. But the work they do, the conditions under which they do it, and for whose benefit are all largely imperceptible to the users of the platforms that pay for and rely upon this labor. In fact, this invisibility is by design.

The goal of this book is therefore to counter that invisibility and to put these workers and the work they do front of mind: to raise awareness about the fraught and difficult nature of such front-line online screening work, but also to give the rest of us the information we need to engage with more detail, nuance, and complexity in conversations about the impact of social media in our interpersonal, civic, and political lives. We cannot do the latter effectively if we do not know, as they say, how the sausage gets made.

The process of identifying and researching the phenomenon of commercial content moderation has connected me with numerous people in a variety of stages of life, from different socio-economic classes, cultural backgrounds, and life experiences. It has necessitated travel to parts of the world previously unfamiliar to me, and has led me to study the work of scholars of the history, politics, and people of places like the Philippines, while also considering the daily realities of people located in rural Iowa. It has made connections for me between Silicon Valley and India, between Canada and Mexico, and among workers who may not have even recognized themselves as peers. It has also necessitated the formulation of theoretical framings and understandings that I use as a navigation tool. I hope to make those connections across time and space for them, and for all of us.

In the United States, using the internet as a means of communication and social connection can be traced to some of its earliest moments, such as when researchers at UCLA in 1969 attempted to transmit a message from one computer node to another connected through ARPANET—the internet's precursor, funded by the United States Department of Defense (the result was a system crash).[2] As the ARPANET evolved into the internet over the next three decades, important and experimental new social spaces grew up as part of the technological innovation in computation and connectivity; these were text-based realms described using exotic, cryptic acronyms like MOO, MUD, and BBS.[3] People used command-line programs, such as "talk," on the Unix operating system to communicate in real time long before anyone had ever heard of texting. They sent messages to one another in a new form called email that, at one time, made up the majority of data transmissions crossing the internet's networks. Others shared news, debated politics, discussed favorite music, and circulated pornography in Usenet news groups. All were virtual communities of sorts, connecting computer users to one another years before the birth of Facebook's founders. Each site of communication developed its own protocols, its own widely accepted practices, its own particular flavor, social norms, and culture.

Because access to internet-connected computers was not commonplace in the first decades of its existence (there was not even a preponderance of personal computers in everyone's home at this time), access to this nascent internet was largely the province of people affiliated with universities or research and development institutes, largely in the United States, and also in Great Britain and northern Europe.[4] Despite the seemingly homogeneous backgrounds of these early users, people found plenty about which to disagree. Political, religious, and social debates, lengthy arguments, insults, trolling, and flame wars all were common in the early days—even as we continue to struggle with these issues online today.

To contend with these challenges, as well as to develop and enforce a sense of community identity in many early internet social spaces, the users themselves often created rules, participation guidelines, behavioral norms, and other forms of self-governance and control, and anointed themselves, or other users, with superuser status that would allow them to enforce these norms from both a social and technological standpoint. In short, these spaces moderated users, behavior, and the material on them. Citing research by Alexander R. Galloway and Fred Turner, I described the early social internet in an encyclopedia entry as follows:

> The internet and its many underlying technologies are highly codified and protocol-reliant spaces with regard to how data are transmitted within it, yet the subject matter and nature of content itself has historically enjoyed a much greater freedom. Indeed, a central claim to the early promise of the internet as espoused by many of its proponents was that it was highly resistant, as a foundational part of both its architecture and ethos, to censorship of any kind. Nevertheless, various forms of content moderation occurred in early online communities. Such content moderation was frequently undertaken by volunteers and was typically based on the enforcement of local rules of engagement around community norms and user behavior. Moderation practices and style therefore developed locally among communities and their participants and could inform the flavor of a given community, from the highly rule-bound to the anarchic: The Bay Area–based online community the WELL famously banned only three users in its first 6 years of existence, and then only temporarily.[5]

With this background in mind, the reader should view the commercial content moderators introduced throughout this book in the context of an internet that is now more than ever fundamentally a site of control, surveillance, intervention, and circulation of information as a commodity. Content moderation activity and practices have grown up, expanded, and become mission-critical alongside the growth of the internet into the global commercial and economic juggernaut that it is today. I have experienced this transformation taking place over the past two decades firsthand, and it has played a central role in my own life, which I will revisit briefly here to provide context for the internet as it exists today, versus what it used to be.

Summer 1994, Madison, Wisconsin

In the summer of 1994, I was an undergraduate at the University of Wisconsin–Madison, pursuing a double major in French and Spanish language and literature. Despite the proclivity for the humanities that I displayed in my choice of academic pursuits, a longtime fascination with computers, coupled with my newfound interest in internet Bulletin Board Systems (BBS), or text-based online communities (accessed from my dorm room over a 14.4 kilobits-per-second modem and tying up the phone line constantly, much to my roommate's annoyance), meant that I possessed just enough computer skills to retire from being a dishwasher in my dorm's basement cafeteria and move into the relatively cushy job of computer lab specialist in the campus's largest and busiest computer lab. Before laptops were affordable or even portable, and prior to ubiquitous Wi-Fi, the lab, on the ground floor of the university's graduate research library, was an impossibly heavily trafficked place. Many of the university's forty thousand undergrads were familiar to me because they had likely, at some point, camped out in front of a workstation in our lab.

One day, I reported for work and caught up with my colleague Roger as he strolled the floor of the lab. We stopped to contemplate a row of Macintosh Quadras (of the famous "pizza box" form factor) as they churned and labored, mostly unsuccessfully, to load something on their screens. The program's interface had a gray background and some kind of icon in the upper corner to indicate loading was in progress, but nothing came up. (In those days, this was more likely caused by a buggy site or a choked network than anything inherent in the computer program that was running.) After a few moments of watching this computational act of futility, I turned to Roger, a computer science major, and asked, "What *is* that?"

"That," he replied, gesturing at the gray screens, "is NCSA Mosaic. It's a World Wide Web browser."

Seeing my blank look, he explained with impatient emphasis, "It's the graphical internet!"

My disdainful response was as instantaneous as a reflex. "Well," I pronounced, with a dismissive hand wave, "that'll never take off. Everyone knows the internet is a purely text-based medium."

With that, I sealed my fate as perhaps the person more wrong about the future of the internet than anyone had ever been before. Shortly thereafter, the graphical internet, in the form of the World Wide Web, or simply the Web, as it came to be known, did take off—to say the least. This changed the experience and culture of personal computing irrevocably. Internet connectivity went from being a niche experience available to a designated few cloistered in universities and international research-and-development facilities, with denizens who were computer and tech geeks, engineers and computer science

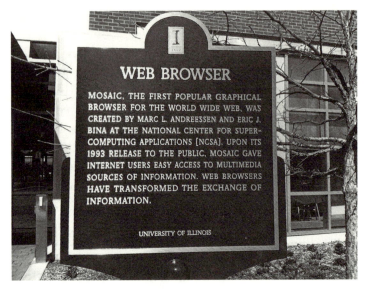

On April 23, 2013, the IEEE Computer Society celebrated the
twentieth anniversary of NCSA Mosaic. This web browser,
developed at the University of Illinois National Center for
Supercomputing Applications (NCSA), was distributed free
of charge, and its graphical user interface, or GUI, and focus
on graphical display of information were largely credited
with sparking widespread interest in and adoption of the
World Wide Web.

majors, to an all-encompassing medium of commerce, communication, finance, employment, entertainment, and social
engagement. Although the internet-fueled tech sector crested
and fell through boom-and-bust cycles over the next two decades, the internet, and the platforms that emerged to exist on
it, became a part of everyday life. Internet access expanded,
going commercial, mobile, and wireless. The American economy became tied to its successes, its excesses, and its crashes.

Meanwhile, my own experience of online life transformed from something I was loath to talk about in mixed company, due to the numerous explanations and excuses I had to make to explain my time spent logged in to something esoteric and unknown. Alongside the increase in local internet service providers (or ISPs) and the ubiquity of America Online starter kits (first on floppy disks and then CD-ROMs), use of the internet as a social and information tool was developing into something more commonplace and understood. In the years that followed, Amazon, Friendster, MySpace, Facebook, and Google brought the internet out of the province of the nerd elite and into everyday life.

I have told the story of my epic prognostication failure numerous times over the years, to colleagues and students alike, using it as a pointed illustration of the dangers of becoming so embedded in one's unique experience of a technology that imagining other iterations, permutations, or ramifications of it becomes impossible. A lack of perspective is dangerously myopic for a technologist, student, or scholar engaged in the study of digital technologies, all identities that I inhabited in the twenty-five years following my initial encounter with NCSA Mosaic. Over the years, I have therefore often avoided making predictions about the ways in which technological developments might or might not transpire or take hold. Yet I return to this story now with a new perspective—one that is somewhat more gracious about the shortcomings of my observations twenty-five years ago. Perhaps what I sensed that summer day in the computer lab was discomfort brought about by a concern for what I felt represented a massive change in how the internet was used and culturally understood.

In 1994, the internet still held, for me, the great promise and potential of a nascent communication form and a powerful information-sharing platform. I found solace in its disembodied nature. It was a place where one could try on different identities, points of view, and political stances. In the social spaces I inhabited online, participants were judged not on how they looked or by their access to material resources, but by how well they constructed their arguments or how persuasively they made a case for the position they advocated. This allowed me, for example, to experiment with identifying as gay well before I was able to do so "IRL" (in real life, in internet parlance). Having had the opportunity to textually partake of the identity made the real-world embodiment much easier than it might have been. What might, therefore, be lost in an internet that was no longer characterized by text, but by image? Even when the public Web was still embryonic, I feared that the change would likely lead to commercialization, and with it, digital enclosure and spaces of control. Indeed, unlike my first and wildly erroneous earlier prediction about the unlikelihood of adoption of the World Wide Web, that one has largely come true.

Even in spite of my own early privileged and mostly positive engagements online, and what I and others viewed as the internet's potential as a space for new ways of thinking and doing, all was not ideal in the pre-commercialization explosion of the Web. Although champions of "cyberspace" (as we poetically referred to it at the time, inspired by William Gibson's cyberpunk fiction) often suggested limitless possibilities for burgeoning internet social communities, their rhetoric frequently evidenced jingoism of a new techno-tribalism, invoking problematic metaphors of techno–Manifest Destiny: pioneering, homesteading, and the electronic frontier.[6]

Other scholars, too, identified a whole host of well-worn real-world "-isms" that appeared in the cyberworld, just as endemic to those spaces, it would seem, as they were in physical space. Lisa Nakamura identified the "hostile performance[s]" of race and gender passing in online textual spaces in her article "Race In/for Cyberspace: Identity Tourism and Racial Passing on the Internet," in 1995. Legal scholar Jerry Kang and sociologist Jessie Daniels have also contributed key theoretical takes on the deployment of racism in the context of online life, despite its being heralded by many proponents as color-blind.[7] By 1998, Julian Dibbell had recounted the bizarre and disturbing tale of anonymity-enabled sexual harassment on LambdaMOO in "A Rape in Cyberspace," the first chapter of his book on emergent internet social experiences, *My Tiny Life,* and Usenet news groups were characterized by arcane, extensive rules for civil participation and self-governance, or by the opposite, hostile flames and disturbing content serving as the raison d'être of a group's existence.[8] By 1999, Janet Abbate was helping us to understand the complexity of the formation of the internet by computer scientists, the U.S. military, and academics, in partnership with industry.[9] Gabriella Coleman has illuminated the important role of hackers and others shaping the internet outside the conscripted boundaries of easily understood legal and social norms.[10]

In 1999, legal scholar Lawrence Lessig burst onto the burgeoning internet studies and cyberlaw scene with his accessible best-selling monograph *Code, and Other Laws of Cyberspace.*[11] In it, he tackled issues of content ownership, copyright, and digital rights from a decidedly pro-user, open-access perspective as they related to the internet. When the open-source movement was taking on greater importance, with successes such as Linux moving from a fringe hobbyists' operating system to a business-ready, enterprise system (such as when RedHat went public) and in the wake of the rise and dramatic fall of Napster, consternation was growing among internet users about the legal perils and liabilities of file-sharing and other kinds of internet use. In his text, Lessig addressed these issues head-on, arguing for greater openness and access to information as a potential source of creativity and innovation. He warned against the dangers of continued encroachment of digital rights management (DRM), media conglomeration, like the then-recent AOL–Time Warner merger, and a variety of moves that he saw as a threat to the free circulation of information on the internet. Others, such as legal scholar Jamie Boyle, discussed the need for expansion and protection of the digital commons, a historical allusion to and metaphor based on the closing of the physical commons of sixteenth-century England.[12]

This fledgling social internet was therefore not without problems, not least because it was a rarefied and privileged space. Yet it was during this early period that everyday use of the internet by commercial entities, government agencies, students, and lay users also began to grow at massive levels. The Pew Research Center's Internet & American Life Project characterized the growth as facilitated by access to three interrelated technology sectors: broadband, mobile internet-enabled devices, and social media platforms. Scholars, including Lessig and Boyle, internet activists, and organizations (such as the Electronic Frontier Foundation, or EFF) focused on concerns over the potential for increased surveillance and control by corporate and government entities, enabled by the very same technologies that allowed Americans to get online and stay online—for work and for leisure—in unprecedented numbers.

Historically, legal jurisdiction had functioned in direct relationship to the geographic and political borders that have defined a particular region or state. These had been commonly understood and recognized by those subject to their laws, thus allowing for consent of the governed necessary for the enforcement of laws. The development of national and international media of various types (such as newspapers and radio) certainly may have challenged the notion of clear-cut borders, but not nearly to the extent and without as much fanfare (or threat) as the internet did in its early transition to a major consumer, commercial, and social media site of engagement.

For many of its proponents, the promise of the early internet was that it knew no geographic boundaries; it seemed to transcend international borders and to exist in a space that was both geographically territory-less and its own distinct location simultaneously. The internet was paradoxically nowhere and everywhere, constituting a brave new borderless world and suggesting, among other things, an untapped and exciting potential to many for access to ideas and speech that, in some areas, was otherwise precluded by the state. Early cyberlibertarian/technologist John Gilmore, for example, was famously quoted as saying that the very architecture of the internet was structurally immune (or at least highly resistant) to any censorship of information, accidental or otherwise, that traveled through its interconnected nodes. Another early internet luminary, John Perry Barlow, famously issued a Declaration of the Independence of Cyberspace that actively challenged and rejected traditional government control, legislation, and jurisdiction over the internet.[13] Large internet companies even claimed that not only was it impractical but it was, in essence, technologically infeasible to attempt to restrict access or content based on users' geographic location (and, hence, their legal jurisdiction)—a claim later famously disproven in a court case that led to geolocation and content limiting based on IP address.[14]

Yet today the vast majority of what most people consider "the internet" is, in fact, the province of private corporations over which they can exercise virtually no control. These companies are often major transnational conglomerates that enjoy close relationships with the governments of their countries of origin. This privatization occurs across all levels of connectivity and access, from the backbones that connect the world's networked computers, of which there are only five major ones (with those second- and third-tier backbones largely in the hands of only a few transnational media or communications conglomerates) providing access to content that is delivered within privately held platforms.[15]

Commercial content moderation is a powerful mechanism of control and has grown up alongside, and in service to, these private concerns that are now synonymous with "the internet." It is part and parcel of the highly regulated, mediated, and commercialized internet of platforms and services owned by private corporations. The practice of it is typically hidden and imperceptible. For the most part, users cannot significantly influence or engage with it, and typically do not know that it is even taking place, themes raised in interviews with current and former commercial content moderators contained in this book. To fully understand the workers' insights, the context provided in this chapter serves as the backdrop to the environment in which all of the workers I spoke to operate.

The narrative contained in this book represents the *first* eight years of a scholarly endeavor, because this work represents the research agenda of a lifetime. Who I am in terms of my own positionality—identities, life experiences, perceptions, and other facets of self—is a key part of the story of what I have uncovered. My own experiences online, which have mirrored the development and adoption of the commercial internet as a part of everyday life, and my subsequent work as an information technologist, have driven my interest in the phenomenon of commercial content moderation and the lives of its workers.

My first experiences with nascent online communities—characterized by tedious and often contentious self-governance, voluntary participation and veneration of status-holding and power-wielding community leaders, predisposition to the primacy of computer geek culture, and DIY sensibilities (it was not uncommon for a system to be hosted, for example, on a cast-off mainframe computer in someone's closet)—have contextualized and framed my approach to my own life online. Years later, my own early experiences were put in sharp relief as I read, for the first time, about a group of Iowa-based content screeners, one state over—people who probably looked very much like me, and whose lives, like mine, revolved around the internet. But in the twenty-five years since I first logged on, the landscape had changed dramatically. Online work has gone from being niche employment for a select Bay Area few to the norm for millions, and the promise of the digital economy was at the center of federal technology and employment policy, as well as the aspiration for many. Commercial content moderation is a job, a function, and an industrial practice that exists only in this context and could only ever exist in it.

Today, important insights into how we perceive the contemporary internet have been made by digital sociologists Jessie Daniels, Karen Gregory, and Tressie McMillan Cottam, as well as researchers from legal, communications, and information studies traditions like Danielle Citron, Joan Donovan, Safiya U. Noble, Sarah Myers West, danah boyd, Siva Vaidhyanathan, Zeynep Tufekci, and Whitney Phillips, among others, who study the impact of online hate, hostility, and the role of social media platforms in fostering ill effects on individuals, societies, and democracies. It is my hope that this book will complement and add to this important dialogue and will serve to both enrich and complicate our understanding of online life today.[16]

Chapter 1 is the tale of when the work of professional internet moderators first significantly came to light beyond the confines of industry, thanks to a key article in the *New York Times,* and my own introduction to it. I recount this moment in 2010 and draw links to other areas of obfuscated human labor and intervention in the internet ecosystem in order to describe the scope and stakes, then and now, for commercial content moderation and its impact.

The concept of commercial content moderation, and contexts in which people undertake this work, are described in detail in Chapter 2. This chapter maps the concept of content moderation contextually and theoretically, and develops a taxonomy of the practice, introducing cases that exemplify the practices and conditions of commercial content moderation. This helps situate it within historical and contemporary discussions of digital labor and the digital economy writ large, providing examples of recent high-profile cases with a concomitant analysis.

Chapter 3 introduces three workers who are employed as contractors in a major Silicon Valley internet giant pseudonymously referred to as MegaTech. Featuring the workers largely in their own words, the chapter describes the workplace culture and daily experiences of contract workers in the Valley environment. The workers speak about the stress and negative effect of their jobs on their lives at work and home. I argue that the workers' insights into the nature of content moderation labor reveal a complex and problematic underside to the social media economy, and to broader notions of internet culture and policy. The workers are remarkably self-aware and perceptive, and the chapter captures the richness of their voices and experiences by including many powerful excerpts from interviews with them, along with my own analysis.

Earlier studies of similar low-wage, low-status fields (for example, call centers) or of work involving screening tasks exist and have proven instructive in framing the analysis for this book. In her study of airport security screeners, Lisa Parks cites a congressional hearing in which work involving relentless searching and screening via video was described as a "repetitive, monotonous and stressful task that requires constant vigilance."[17] In the case of content moderators, not only is their work likely to be monotonous, but it also frequently exposes them to disturbing images whose hazards go unnoticed because they are not necessarily physically apparent, immediate, or understood.

Following the focus on contractors at Silicon Valley's MegaTech, Chapter 4 returns to the work lives of moderators in two additional and distinct contexts: one working in, and managing, a boutique social media specialty firm and another supplying contract labor for an online digital news site. Workers featured in this chapter contribute important insights into their specific contexts, elucidating both the divisions in commercial content moderation as it is undertaken in distinct organizational contexts while drawing links among experiences and observations among people who do this work worldwide.

In Chapter 5, I focus on the work and life of a group of moderators in Manila, Philippines. In 2013, the Philippines surpassed India, at a fraction of its size in population, as the call center capital of the world. Filipino workers, much like others who work in call center environments globally, must perform cultural and linguistic competencies every day as they vet content originating in and destined for very different parts of the world from where they are located. This chapter offers the comparative case of commercial content moderation in the Philippines to argue that this phenomenon, as outsourced to the Global South, is a practice predicated on long-standing relationships of Western cultural, military, and economic domination that social media platforms exploit for inexpensive, abundant, and culturally competent labor. It describes the experiences of five Filipino content screeners, in their own words against a historical and contemporary backdrop that familiarizes the reader with their work life in modern Manila.

In Chapter 6, the book concludes with an informed yet speculative look toward the future of content moderation and the future of digital work in general. It discusses where commercial content moderation practices may be heading, in terms of regulation and other pressures on social media firms for greater accountability and transparency. It also addresses platforms' claims of the ability of artificial intelligence to supersede human moderation. I argue that while social media firms may no longer be able to conceal the active intervention of content moderation workers, it is not clear that merely bringing their activities into the light will result in a better workplace environment or improved status. I suggest that this hidden cost of social media use may well be endemic to the platforms, with a bill that will come due at some point in the future in the form of damaged workers and an even more frightening social media landscape. This chapter closes with an overview of the current state of commercial content moderation, including legal and policy developments in a number of European countries, such as Germany, Belgium, and Austria, and at the European Union level, that push back on major platforms' unilateral management of content moderation; discussion of landmark lawsuits involving commercial content management workers at Microsoft and now at Facebook; and an analysis of the implications of the larger social uptake and public consciousness of commercial content management.

Behind the Screen is a long-form overview of the commercial content moderation phenomenon that cuts in at the level of the personal, focusing on work lives of those who implement social media policy and who are on the front lines. It is long in its gestation and covers significant chronological and theoretical ground, but it is not a definitive or final statement. Rather, it enters into a dialog under way in the hopes of complementing extant work by a variety of academics and advocates focused on commercial content moderation, specifically, and content moderation in general. That dialog includes voices concerned with content moderation and legal perspectives, human rights and freedom of expression, platform governance and accountability, the future of the internet, among many other points of view. Key works in this area are published or forthcoming by Kate Klonick, James Grimmelmann, Tarleton Gillespie, Sarah Myers West, Nikos Smyrnaiois and Emmanuel Marty, Nora A. Draper, Claudia Lo, Karen Frost Arnold, Hanna Bloch-Wehba, Kat Lo, and many others.[18] My own thinking and conceptualizing have been greatly enriched by their work, and I encourage all interested readers to seek it out.

1

Behind the Screen

Summer 2010, Champaign, Illinois

During the hot and muggy summer of 2010, iced latte in one hand, I idly clicked my way through the *New York Times* online. It was a welcome, fleeting break from my doctoral studies at the Graduate School of Library and Information Science at the University of Illinois. A public land grant institution, the university dominates the economy and geography of the small twin towns of Urbana and Champaign that yield at the towns' perimeter to endless cornfields on all sides. That part of Illinois is precarious to the health of anyone with seasonal allergies or put off by agricultural scenes.

I was spending the summer there, in oppressive heat and humidity, working as a teaching assistant and doing an independent study on digital media. Taking a break from grading and course prep, I dipped into my brief daily diversion, perusing the news stories. A small story relegated to the Tech section of the paper, "Concern for Those Who Screen the Web for Barbarity," commanded my attention.[1]

The reporter, Brad Stone, set the stage: a call center company called Caleris, providing business process outsourcing

(BPO) services in a similarly agricultural and nearby Iowa town, had branched into a new kind of service.[2] Content screening, or content moderation, was a practice wherein hourly-wage employees reviewed uploaded user-generated content (UGC)—the photos, videos, and text postings all of us create on social media platforms—for major internet sites. The *New York Times* piece focused on the fact that the Caleris workers, and those at a few other content moderation centers in the United States, were suffering work-related burnout triggered by the disturbing images and video they were reviewing. This material often included scenes of obscenity, hate speech, abuse of children and of animals, and raw and unedited war-zone footage.

Some other firms specializing in content screening, the article stated, had begun offering psychological counseling to employees who found themselves disturbed and depressed by the material they were viewing. For a mere eight dollars per hour, workers were subjected to disturbing content that users had uploaded to social media platforms or websites. The material was so upsetting that many employees eventually pursued psychological counseling. As I read the article, it became clear how this new type of tech employment would be a necessity for social media platforms, or for any companies asking for feedback or a review of their product on the open Web. The need for brand protection alone was compelling: no company would want to solicit content from unknown and generally anonymous internet users without a means to intervene over objectionable, unflattering, or illegal material that might be posted. Yet, despite almost twenty years, at that point, of active participation online as a user, information technology worker, and ultimately internet researcher, until that moment in 2010 I had never heard of such workers or even imagined that they existed in an organized, for-pay way such as this.

I forwarded the article to a number of friends, colleagues, and professors, all longtime internet users like me, and digital media and internet scholars themselves. "Have you heard of this job?" I asked. "Do you know anything about this kind of work?" None of them had, although a few had also seen the *Times* story before I sent it to them. They, too, were transfixed. For a bunch of net nerds and digital media geeks, we knew shockingly next to nothing about this practice, which I came to call commercial content moderation—to differentiate this labor from the familiar types of volunteer governance and self-policing activities that had commonly been performed in online spaces and communities for years.

Yet, once I gave it significant thought, it seemed obvious that such a practice must exist on commercial platforms that rely on user-generated content to draw and sustain audiences. In 2014, users uploaded more than one hundred hours of video per minute to YouTube alone. Far surpassing the reach of any cable network, YouTube disseminated its content to billions around the globe. By 2015, YouTube uploads had increased to four hundred hours per minute, with one billion hours of content viewed daily as of 2017.[3] By 2013, news outlets reported that 350 million images per day were being uploaded to Facebook.[4] Over the past decade, the increase in scope, reach, and economics of these platforms and their concomitant labor and material impacts have been traced in influential works by scholars such as Nick Dyer-Witheford, Jack Linchuan Qiu, Antonio Casilli, Miriam Posner, and many others.[5] By 2018, simple math based on the number of user-content-reliant social media platforms and other content-sharing mechanisms in the marketplace—such as Snapchat, Instagram, One Drive, Dropbox, WhatsApp, and Slack—by a rough estimate of their user bases, or the amount of content generated per day, makes it clear that handling such an influx has to be a major and unending concern, with a massive global workforce to contend with it and a massive global supply chain of network cables, mineral mining, device production, sales, software development, data centers, and e-waste disposal to support it.

When I read that article in 2010, neither YouTube nor Facebook had been so widely adopted yet by users. Nevertheless, even by that point those platforms and their mainstream online peers had already captured audiences of hundreds of millions worldwide, delivering ever-updated content to them in exchange for their eyeballs, clicks, and attention to partner advertising running next to their hosted videos and images. It stood to reason that the YouTubes, Facebooks, Twitters, and Instagrams of the world would not simply let content flow unfettered over their branded properties without some form of gatekeeping. But, as I reflected at greater length, notwithstanding the lack of public discussion about the platforms' filtering practices, it seemed obvious that decisions made by content screeners working in obscurity in office cubicles had the potential to markedly affect the experience of the users who created most of the content on these platforms.

Judgments related to social norms and cultural aesthetics, content curation, and compliance with internal site guidelines and external, overarching laws were being administered by some of the lowest-paid workers at the companies, who were, at the same time, being exposed to harm in that process. These workers existed behind the screen, anonymous and unknown. Who were they? Where did they work and under what conditions? What was their work life like? What decisions were they being charged with, and for whose benefit did they make them? And, most important to me, why were we not collectively talking about them, about the work they did and its impact on them, and on the internet so many of us consume and where so many of us spend our lives?

The pursuit of answers to those questions has sustained, driven, and frustrated me for eight years, taken me on a trajectory around the world, from North America to Europe to the Philippine megalopolis of Manila. It has put me in contact with workers, management, advocates, artists, and attorneys; put me periodically at odds with powerful firms and entities and at other times in the same room; and given me a voice with which to speak about the realities of commercial content moderation work to audiences small and large.

The Hidden Digital Labor of Commercial Content Moderation

After years of obscurity, commercial content moderation and the material realities of what the employees performing this work have to endure have more recently made international headlines. In the wake of the 2016 American presidential election, the role of social media platforms and the information they circulate online has been questioned by a public concerned, for the first time in significant numbers, about the way social media content is produced. The term "fake news" has been introduced into the general discourse. In 2017, commercial content moderation became a hot topic after a series of highly publicized and violent, tragic events were broadcast, in some cases live to the world, on Facebook and other social media platforms. These events raised questions in the public sphere about what and how material circulates online and who, if anyone, is doing the gatekeeping.

To the surprise of much of the public, as it was to me in 2010, we now know that much of the labor of these adjudication processes on platforms is undertaken not by sophisticated artificial intelligence and deep learning algorithms, but by poorly paid human beings who risk burnout, desensitization, and worse because of the nature of their work. Facebook, YouTube and other huge tech platforms have been beset by leaks in the pages of major newspapers from disgruntled content moderators eager to make the public aware of their role and their working conditions, and the limitations and impact of social media and algorithms are increasingly studied by computer and social scientists and researchers, such as Taina Bucher, Virginia Eubanks, Safiya Noble, and Meredith Broussard.[6]

After so many years in the shadows, it seems that the phenomenon of commercial content moderation—the intertwined systems of the outsourcing firms that supply the labor, the giant platforms that require it, and the people who perform the filtering tasks that keep so many vile images and messages away from users' screens—is having a moment. That the topic has seized the public's consciousness across academic, journalistic, technological, and policy-making sectors has come largely in spite of continued opacity, obfuscation, and general unwillingness to discuss it on the part of social media firms that rely on these practices to do business.

To penetrate the tech corporations' stonewalling about the cloaked interventions they make that determine what you ultimately see on your screen, I realized that I would have to get in touch with the moderators themselves. Locating the moderators, and persuading them to speak about their work in light of the legal restrictions placed on them by their employers, has been challenging but crucially important. The process has been complicated by the job insecurity of many content screeners, the barrier of nondisclosure agreements, which they are typically compelled to sign, and the term-limited positions that cause them to cycle in and out of the workforce. An additional challenge was their multiple locations within a worldwide network of outsourcing firms that sees flows of digital labor tasks circumnavigate the globe under many monikers and far removed from the platforms ultimately reliant upon them.

Throughout the interview process, I took pains not to exacerbate the difficult experiences of commercial content monitors by asking sensationalistic or voyeuristic questions, but instead posed interview questions crafted with care designed to allow the workers to express what they felt was most important about their work and lives. I have been eager to share the importance of their work, their own insights and awareness, with a larger audience. This empirical research, with content moderation workers themselves, and my subsequent analysis and reflections have evolved into this book.

Over time, my research and its outcomes have shifted and evolved, as have the aims of the book, which are multiple. Aad Blok, in his introduction to *Uncovering Labour in Information Revolutions, 1750–2000,* notes that scholarly discussions of the evolutions and revolutions in information and communication technology have tended to ignore the concomitant developments in labor practices. He further notes that if "in this respect, any attention is given to labour, it is focused mainly on the highly skilled 'knowledge work' of inventors, innovators, and system-builders."[7] This book aims to avoid such an oversight in the case of commercial content moderation workers by instead foregrounding their contributions alongside other knowledge work that is typically better known and accorded higher status. Recent years have seen many new and important additions to the critical literature on new forms of labor necessitated or predicated upon the increasing reliance on the digital, with many important new studies on the horizon.

I subsequently make the case for what this type of moderation work can tell us about the current state of the internet, and what the internet is actually in the business of. Indeed, if there is a central argument upon which this book hinges, it is my belief that any discussion of the nature of the contemporary internet is fundamentally incomplete if it does not address the processes by which certain content created by users is allowed to remain visible and other content is removed, who makes these decisions, how they are made, and whom they benefit. Indeed, the content screeners I spoke with recognize the centrality of their work in creating the contemporary social media landscape that, as users, we typically take for granted, as if the content on it must be there by design, because it is "best," has been vetted, or has inherent value. The moderators themselves tell a different story. Their tale is often a paradoxical one, characterized by the difficult and demanding work they do to curb the flow of problematic, objectionable, and illegal material, all the while knowing that they are touching only a drop in the bucket of the billions of monetized videos, images, and streams connecting us to one another, and delivering us to advertisers, on social media platforms.

Ghosts in the Machine: On Human Traces in Digital Systems

A certain myopia characterizes collective engagement with social media platforms and the user-created content they solicit and disseminate. These platforms have long traded on a predominating origin myth of unfettered possibility for democratic free expression, on one hand, and a newer concept of unidirectional, direct user-to-platform-to-dissemination media creation opportunities offered by "Web 2.0" and social media platforms, on the other (witness YouTube's on-again, off-again slogan, "Broadcast Yourself"). And yet, the existence of commercial content moderation workers and the practices they engage in certainly challenge the end user's perceived relationship to the social media platform to which she or he is uploading content. For end users, that relationship is a simple one: they upload content and it appears to the world. In reality, the content is subject to an ecosystem made up of intermediary practices, policies, and people whose agendas, motivations, allegiances—and mere existence—are likely imperceptible and therefore not taken into account when that user clicks "upload."

But once the existence of these intermediary agents becomes known, what else might be up for reevaluation? What other practices are worthy of another critical glance to identify the human values and actions embedded within them, and how does recognition of them change our understandings of them? In her book *Algorithms of Oppression,* Safiya U. Noble demonstrates how Google's search function structures harmful representations of gender, sexuality, and race.[8] Miriam Sweeney asks questions about the nature of human intervention and embedded value systems in the creation of computerized digital assistants known as anthropomorphized virtual agents, or AVAs.[9] Rena Bivens documents in a ten-year study the impact of the gender binary in Facebook, and its ramifications for gender expression and choice.[10] Whose values do these platforms actually reflect? Whom do these tools and systems depict, how and to what end?

Critical interventions intended to complicate or unveil the politics and humanity of digital technology are present at the nexus of art, activism, and scholarship. Andrew Norman

Wilson, one such person working at that intersection, has sought to show human traces within digital processes by revealing the literal handiwork of Google Book scanners. As a one-time Google-contracted videographer, he noticed a building on the Google campus that a group of workers streamed into and out of at odd hours of the day, segregated from the rest of those located on Google's sprawling property in Mountain View, California. He learned that these workers were contracted to produce the millions of page scans needed for Google's massive book digitization project—a project that, in its final production-ready iteration, betrays no sign of these human actors involved in its creation. When Wilson probed too deeply into the lesser working conditions and status of the scanners, he was fired, and Google attempted to confiscate the video recording he had made of the workers, which, in homage to the cinematic and documentary endeavors of the Lumière Brothers' *Workers Leaving the Lumière Factory* in 1895, he titled *Workers Leaving the Googleplex*.[11] In this way, he linked the status and work conditions of the book scanners on Google's campus directly to those of factory workers—a much less glamorous proposition than work at Google is generally depicted as being.

It is the erasure of these human traces, both literally and in a more abstract sense, that is so fascinating, and we must constantly ask to whose benefit such erasures serve. As for the Google book scanners, their human traces have been revealed, preserved, and celebrated as a sort of found art, through the work of Wilson, as well as through a popular Tumblr blog created by an MFA student at the Rhode Island School of Design (and even lauded in that bastion of American highbrow culture the *New Yorker*).[12] The Tumblr blog presents a veneration of Google Books errata that is both entertaining and thought-provoking, revealing everything from fingers caught in the act of scanning to notes in the margins to scanning misfires that result in new permutations of texts.[13]

Wilson's work and the Tumblr blog, however, still reveal not much more than a hint of the human trace behind what most people assume is an automated process. Both still leave us in the dark about who made the traces and under what conditions.

In Closure

As individuals and, on a larger scale, as societies, we are ceding unprecedented amounts of control to private companies, which see no utility or benefit to providing transparent access to their technologies, architectures, practices, or finances. It becomes difficult, if not impossible, to truly know and be able to hold accountable those we engage to provide critical informational services. The full extent of their reach, their practices with the data and content we generate for them, and the people who engage with these materials are almost always unknown to and unknowable by us. By dint of this opaque inaccessibility, these digital sites of engagement—social media platforms, information systems, and so on—take on an oracle-like mysticism, becoming, as Alexander Halavais calls them, "object[s] of faith."[14]

Yet technologies are never neutral, and therefore are not "naturally" benign or without impact. On the contrary, they are, by their nature as sociotechnical constructions, at once reflective of their creators while also being created in the service of something or someone—whether as designed, or when as reimagined or repurposed in acts of adaptation or acts of resistance. This fact therefore begs for a thorough interrogation of the questions "Who benefits?" and "What are the ramifications of the deployment and adoption of these technologies for the accumulation and expansion of power, acculturation, marginalization, and capital?" We know, for example, that the histories of technological development have been subject to structural exclusion of women, as historian Mar Hicks documents in her work on the purposeful exclusion of women from computer programming in the United Kingdom, which subsequently eroded the potency of the British in the global rise of computing.[15] Similarly, systematic racial and gender discrimination at AT&T in the United States adversely impacted the bourgeoning Black and Latina workforce, precluding these early tech workers from meaningful long-term careers in telephony, computing, and technology, as chronicled by scholars Venus Green and Melissa Villa-Nicholas.[16]

Social media platforms, digital protocols, and computer architecture are all human constructs and human pursuits, embedded with human choices and reflecting human values. Media scholar Lev Manovich poses this challenge: "As we work with software and use the operations embedded in it, these operations become part of how we understand ourselves, others, and the world. Strategies of working with computer data become our general cognitive strategies. At the same time, the design of software and the human-computer interface reflects a larger social logic, ideology, and imaginary of the contemporary society. So if we find particular operations dominating software programs, we may also expect to find them at work in the culture at large."[17]

Many scholars and activists, such as those cited and discussed here, have dedicated great amounts of intellectual labor and written words to questioning the practices and the policies that render systems opaque and that result in our information as commodities in the digital system. Less is known, though, about the human actors who labor as intermediaries in these systems. After all, activists, scholars, and users can address only what they can see and know, or at least imagine, and what they can engage with. This introduction to the broad issues surrounding commercial content moderation is, therefore, intended to contextualize some of the conditions of the contemporary internet: its histories, its affordances, and its absences. Commercial content moderators are intermediaries who negotiate an internet defined in the terms discussed here; they manipulate and referee (frequently in secret) user-generated content in social media platforms to the end of creating spaces that are more palatable, accessible, and inviting, and that elicit more user participation. They do so for money, and they do so in terms of the goals and benefits of the companies that engage their services. While a better user experience may be an outcome of the work they do, this is always, and ultimately, because that better experience benefits the company providing the space for participation online.

2

Understanding Commercial Content Moderation

As we have seen, commercial content moderation is the organized practice of screening user-generated content posted to internet sites, social media, and other online outlets. The activity of reviewing user-generated content may take place before the material is submitted for inclusion or distribution on a site, or it may take place after material has already been uploaded. In particular, content screening may be triggered as a result of complaints about material from site moderators or other site administrators, from external parties (for example, companies alleging misappropriation of material they own), or from other users who are disturbed or concerned by what they have seen and then trigger mechanisms on a site, an action called the "flagging" of content, to prompt a review by professional moderators.[1]

Commercial content moderation is an essential practice in the production cycle for commercial websites, social media platforms, and media properties that solicit content from users as a part of their online presence. For the companies employing this practice, moderation and screening are crucial steps that protect their corporate or platform brand (by enforcing user adherence to site guidelines or rules), ensure compliance with the laws and statutes governing their operations, and contribute positively to maintaining an audience of users willing to upload and view content on their sites.

Yet the process to handle this content is often catch-as-catch-can. On many highly trafficked sites, the amount of user-generated content submitted is staggering—and growing. Issues of scale aside, the complex process of sorting user-uploaded material into either the acceptable or the rejected pile is far beyond the capabilities of software or algorithms alone. Not just a technical or computational issue, the long history of theoretical challenges in sorting and classifying information has been well documented by scholars like Geoffrey Bowker and Susan Leigh Star and is the starting point for the challenge of content moderation of this scope and volume.[2] It is where the nature of the content (that is, what it is or what it depicts), its intent (that is, what it is meant to do when consumed or circulated), its unintended consequences (that is, what else it might do, beyond its first-order intent), and its meaning (which can be highly specific, culturally, regionally, or otherwise) all intersect. From there, it must then be evaluated against "the rules," both of the platform or local context of the ecosystem (its social norms, expectations, tolerances, and mores) and of the larger, open world and *its* social, cultural, commercial, and legal regimes and mandates.

Some content lends itself to partial batch processing or other types of machine-automated filtering, particularly when that material is extant and already resident in databases of known bad material. But given the complexity of these processes and the many issues that must be weighed and balanced all at once, the vast majority of social media content uploaded by its users requires human intervention for it to be appropriately screened—particularly where video or images are involved. Human screeners are called upon to employ an array of high-level cognitive functions and cultural competencies to make decisions about their appropriateness for a site or platform. Importantly, for most mainstream social media platforms that rely on user participation, the norm is to allow all uploads without significant pre-screening, meaning that, with a few exceptions, any adjudication or decision making about the appropriateness of a particular video, image, or text post will likely come after it has already been on the platform for some period of time. This paradigm was a business decision on the part of the social media companies themselves, and certainly not a foregone conclusion based on technological necessity or other factors. It is one that users have now typically come to expect.

Professional moderators must be experts in matters of taste of the site's presumed audience and have cultural knowledge about the location where the platform is based and the platform's audience. Both the headquarters of the tech platform and its audience may be very far removed, geographically and culturally, from the location where workers are viewing and moderating the user-generated content. Moderators must have linguistic competency in the language of the content (which may be a learned or second language for the screener), be steeped in the relevant laws governing the site's country of origin, and have expert knowledge of user guidelines and other incredibly detailed platform-level specifics concerning what is and is not allowed.

Some material uploaded by users is inappropriate based on general site guidelines, or under the law. In such cases, moderators

Don't cross the line

Here are some common-sense rules that'll help you steer clear of trouble. Please take these rules seriously and take them to heart. Don't try to look for loopholes or try to lawyer your way around the guidelines—just understand them and try to respect the spirit in which they were created.

Nudity or sexual content
YouTube is not for pornography or sexually explicit content. If this describes your video, even if it's a video of yourself, don't post it on YouTube. Also, be advised that we work closely with law enforcement and we report child exploitation. Learn more

Harmful or dangerous content
Don't post videos that encourage others to do things that might cause them to get badly hurt, especially kids. Videos showing such harmful or dangerous acts may get age-restricted or removed depending on their severity. Learn more

Violent or graphic content
It's not okay to post violent or gory content that's primarily intended to be shocking, sensational, or disrespectful. If posting graphic content in a news or documentary context, please be mindful to provide enough information to help people understand what's going on in the video. Don't encourage others to commit specific acts of violence. Learn more

Copyright
Respect copyright. Only upload videos that you made or that you're authorized to use. This means don't upload videos you didn't make, or use content in your videos that someone else owns the copyright to, such as music tracks, snippets of copyrighted programs, or videos made by other users, without necessary authorizations. Visit our Copyright Center for more information.

Hateful content
Our products are platforms for free expression. But we don't support content that promotes or condones violence against individuals or groups based on race or ethnic origin, religion, disability, gender, age, nationality, veteran status, or sexual orientation/gender identity, or whose primary purpose is inciting hatred on the basis of these core characteristics. This can be a delicate balancing act, but if the primary purpose is to attack a protected group, the content crosses the line. Learn more

Threats
Things like predatory behavior, stalking, threats, harassment, intimidation, invading privacy, revealing other people's personal information, and inciting others to commit violent acts or to violate the Terms of Use are taken very seriously. Anyone caught doing these things may be permanently banned from YouTube. Learn more

Spam, misleading metadata, and scams
Everyone hates spam. Don't create misleading descriptions, tags, titles, or thumbnails in order to increase views. It's not okay to post large amounts of untargeted, unwanted or repetitive content, including comments and private messages. Learn more

Screenshot of a portion of a YouTube page describing material prohibited for users to upload, offering insights into the kinds of video that CCM employees must screen out. These guidelines have morphed over the years. As shown here in July 2017, they appealed to users' "common sense" to not "cross the line." YouTube states that it draws the line at graphic and violent content, and also copyright infringement. The former is allowed, the guidelines note, if necessary for a "news or documentary context."

can make quick and easy decisions about it. They may cull their queues of user-generated material by engaging computational tools like automated text searches for banned words (to moderate text-based comment sections), "skin filters" to determine if a large portion of an image or video shows bare flesh (suggesting, but not always indicating, pornography), or tools designed to match, flag, or remove copyrighted material.[3] Yet even when aided by these mechanisms that may speed up or even automate aspects of the moderation process, the vast amount of uploaded user content has typically required human evaluation and review, particularly when flagged by other users.

In the case of images and video, machine-automated detection remains an incredibly complex computational problem. The subfield known as "computer vision"—computer recognition of images and objects—is an ongoing area of research that presents numerous technological challenges, frequently making it computationally and financially infeasible to implement across the board and at scale in many content moderation environments.[4] These tasks therefore fall to humans who work through queues of digital material, employing their own decision-making process and, if necessary, intervention.

Whether undertaken through computational or human means, or likely through some combination thereof, the organized, professional full-time work of moderating user-generated content has been a relatively unknown and frequently not-fully-disclosed aspect of participation in social media and websites and services that rely on user-generated content. Many online social media sites and other platforms that trade in user-uploaded material consider the detailed internal-facing specifics of their moderation practices and their policies to be proprietary information. In their view, full disclosure of the exact nature of their policies could lead to unscrupulous users attempting to game the rules, or potentially give business competitors an edge by revealing practices or processes considered secret. The maintaining of these policies as proprietary and secret has also allowed the firms to escape scrutiny and public review of these policies from their users, civil society advocates, and regulators alike. Indeed, content moderators are frequently required to sign nondisclosure agreements (NDAs) about the nature of their work.

For companies whose profits depend on material generated by users, there is, however, at least one other factor that encourages them to keep their content moderation practices veiled. They have viewed their need for large-scale, industrialized content moderation as an unpleasant necessity, that, were it known and fully understood, would have the potential to reveal an underside of sites as mechanisms of distribution for users wishing to circulate unpleasant, distasteful, and disturbing material—not the image most mainstream platforms are eager to cultivate. These platforms therefore engage commercial content moderators to perform tasks that oscillate between the mind-numbingly repetitive and mundane to exposure to images and material that can be violent, disturbing, and, at worst, psychologically damaging. Further, under current regimes that have been largely dictated by the social media firms requiring commercial content moderation, these tasks are demanded of workers who are frequently relatively low-status and low-wage in relation to others in the tech industry and sometimes even in the same building.

The reality of the working conditions of commercial content moderators and their necessity to the infrastructure of online participation offers an unpleasant behind-the-curtain vision that few social media companies or other platforms and sites soliciting user-uploaded content care to openly discuss. While reporting on an early news story focusing on the practice of industrial-scale content moderation, Rebecca Hersher of

NPR's *All Things Considered* was denied access to both Microsoft and Google employees. Instead, for her report from 2013, "Laboring in the Shadows to Keep the Web Free of Child Porn," a Microsoft spokesperson, in a significant understatement, described content moderation work as "a yucky job."[5]

To understand the practice of commercial content moderation, it is necessary to gain a picture of how, where, and by whom the work of moderation takes place. Content moderation or screening of social media is part of a production cycle of analytical work that, according to Michael Hardt and Antonio Negri, "creates immaterial products, such as knowledge, information, communication, a relationship, or an emotional response."[6] This social media production is, in turn, facilitated by digital networks in a globally connected environment, arrangements that media studies scholar Michelle Rodino-Colocino describes as "technomadic."[7]

One of my first key discoveries as I researched industrial-scale moderation work for social media was that the work itself is fractured organizationally and geographically, a fact that was not well known or understood, even by those in the industry itself. Commercial content moderators, I realized, labor under a number of different regimes, employment statuses, and workplace conditions around the world—often by design. Frequently, they are deployed far away from the physical locations where the content they moderate is created, and also at great distance from the hosting sites of the platforms for which the material is destined. Their work titles often differ, ranging from "content moderator," to "screener," to "community manager," to a host of other labels that may sometimes be euphemistic, fanciful, or imply little about their expected job activities—let alone their relation to others doing similar work. In fact, even the workers themselves have difficulty recognizing one another by job title alone. Indeed, because the job titles they toil under are so multitudinous and the job sites so dispersed, it is difficult for researchers, reporters, and labor advocates to locate and identify commercial content moderation workers. Journalists like Julia Angwin, Olivia Solon, Davey Alba, and others, however, have worked tirelessly to overcome these barriers to examine the corporate practices of companies like Facebook and Google, and their networks of labor relationships for moderation tasks.[8]

Rather than occurring in a monolithic and easily definable workplace or as a set of work practices, commercial content moderation crosses several industrial sectors. It manifests in a variety of worksites and under working conditions that vary with regard to status and worker relationship to the platform and firm ultimately in need of the gatekeeping practice. The Caleris workers in Iowa, for example, were laboring in what was, for all intents and purposes, a third-party call center. As I tracked job listings and labor markets for digital or information work, I found that workers doing what appeared to be commercial content moderation were distributed globally in places like India, Ireland, and the Philippines. Later in my research I encountered workers employed on site at the headquarters of a major tech firm I refer to as "MegaTech." And I discovered job postings on microlabor platforms like Amazon Mechanical Turk looking to hire people for what they called "content review tasks," yet another term for commercial content moderation. The landscape was varied and complex, requiring theoretical and geographic mapping.

To get an idea of these intricate structures and relationships, I have created a taxonomy of the locations and employment conditions that are typical for most content moderation workers (Table 1). I define four basic types of work situations for professional moderators: in-house, boutiques, call centers, and microlabor websites.

Table 1. Taxonomy of Online Content Moderation Labor Arrangements

Type	Worksite location	Employment characteristics	Employment status
In-house	On-site or in-house at company requiring user-generated content screening and moderation.	Workers are specialized and focus on content screening for a particular site, brand, or platform. Typically offers best wages of all the arrangements for moderation workers, yet frequently at a status less than full-time, permanent full-status work. Likely to be working in a "Trust & Safety" or "Community Operations" division at the firms that have them.	Variable; runs gamut from full-time full employee to limited-term or part-time contracted employment via a third-party company. Workers may be salaried or hourly.
Boutique	Variable; can be local to the boutique firm or done via globally dispersed	Firms specialize in online brand management and content moderation for other firms. They are specialists in managing and	Variable, from full-time permanent employment by the boutique firm to per-job contract work basis.

(*continued*)

Table 1. (*continued*)

Type	Worksite location	Employment characteristics	Employment status
	contractors hired for the screening tasks. Boutique firms may have both.	staying abreast of many areas of a company's online presence; typically engaged by companies that are not digital media companies themselves.	
Call center	Large-scale operations centers with technological infrastructure to handle multiple international clients or contracts and to provide numerous services, often on a 24/7 business cycle.	Third-party companies offering a suite of services (business process outsourcing), among which user-generated content moderation is but one of many call center and other customer-support operations. Located throughout the world. The Philippines is currently the global leader in call centers.	Workers are typically employed by the call center for which they work, which, in turn, secures contracts or subcontracts from major firms. Working conditions and rates of pay vary throughout the globe. In the United States, call center work is typically relatively low-paying hourly work.

Type	Worksite location	Employment characteristics	Employment status
Microlabor platform	Worldwide; online.	Geographically dispersed; workers are disconnected and disjointed from other workers and those soliciting the moderation. Tasks can be done at any time of the day anywhere a worker can access the microlabor website.	Workers' relationship to employers is on a per-task basis; moderation tasks are broken out to their smallest component parts—typically payment per item viewed or screened in a process that can be described as "digital piecework." Compensation is often on the order of pennies per task completed. Workers likely do not know with certainty for whom they are doing moderation or for what platform or purpose their moderation is being undertaken.

The first type is "in-house," a complex concept in the context of online content screening. It can denote a range of employment statuses and relationships to the company and platform or site for which the moderation is being performed. It might connote full-time employment with the company/site or other, less permanent arrangements. Some examples might include workers who perform their moderation labor at the company's physical site (such as a headquarters or company-owned property) alongside other workers, but possess a status other than full-time employee of that company. Their employment status may take forms like "temporary" or "contract," where workers are hired by the platform requiring content moderation, but for a delimited period and with no guaranteed future employment within the company after the contract has been fulfilled.

Another "in-house" arrangement might have workers working on site at the company in need of moderation, but with these workers being hired, managed, and paid by a third-party contracting company or companies. This contracting arrangement is fairly common in the information technology (IT) industry for low- or entry-level positions, or for fixed-term positions, which is how many content moderation jobs are classified.[9] The primary characteristic of "in-house" moderators is that they are physically located at the platform or company for which the screened content is ultimately destined, although very little can be surmised about their employment status with that company based on their physical presence on site alone. On-site commercial content moderators are likely to be found in divisions with names like "Trust & Safety" or "Community Operations" at the firms that have them, including Facebook, Twitter, YouTube, and Snap, among many others.

Second, a "boutique" arrangement refers to specialized firms that offer social media brand management, generally, or content moderation specifically, for other firms. These businesses are specialists in managing and staying abreast of many areas of a company's online presence, and they are typically engaged by client companies that are not digital media or technology companies themselves. Although these clients do not themselves specialize in social media and are not primarily engaged in encouraging user-generated content creation or distribution as a fundamental facet of their business or operations, they employ features (for example, comments sections, user picture uploads) that solicit such content to encourage customer or citizen engagement and loyalty. This content requires monitoring, screening, and moderation.

In recent years, companies like the U.K.-based eModeration (now known as "The Social Element") or the highly stylized California-based ModSquad have provided these specialized services. Such companies may manage brand identity across numerous online platforms and sites, including the company's own website, Twitter accounts, Facebook pages, and so on.[10] In many cases, not only do they moderate and curate engagement with user-generated content on behalf of other companies, they may even engage in "community management" practices: seeding content by posting comments, tweeting, or otherwise attempting to engage consumers in positive conversations or interactions regarding brands or products of the companies for which they work. OnlineExperts, a boutique firm described in detail in Chapter 4, is an exemplar of this arrangement.

Third, I define the "call center" environment as third-party companies offering a suite of services (frequently referred to as business process outsourcing, or BPO), among which moderation of user-generated content is but one service, and is often secondary to call center and other customer-support operations. These companies have the benefit of already being highly technologically enhanced, a necessary feature in order to handle globalized high-volume phone or data traffic; the addition of content moderation work can therefore be passed along to them with ease and efficiency. These centers are globally dispersed, with many call centers now based in the Philippines, although many others are located in India, Bangladesh, and other regions of the world (including the United States, Ireland, and Italy).[11] These centers rely on a multilingual and multiculturally competent workforce that works on site at the call center to respond to the labor needs of a global marketplace, often on a 24/7 cycle. In call center environments catering to Western business needs that are themselves located outside the West, issues of cultural and linguistic authenticity can serve as mechanisms for firms to differentiate themselves and to suggest a higher level of service. Workers in these environments are asked to perform linguistic and cultural norms that match those of the clientele, but which are often at odds with their own local cultural and linguistic self-expression. This disconnect can result in the translation of a job well done into measures of how good an employee may be at cultural and linguistic passing.[12]

The fourth and final type I identify is "microlabor websites." Content moderation as microlabor digital piecework has been perhaps an obvious site of expansion for globally networked microlabor websites. These digital labor marketplaces connect parties seeking task completion and those seeking employment on a per-task or per-job basis. Sites such as Upwork (formerly oDesk.com) and Amazon Mechanical Turk allow workers to solicit knowledge work tasks that can be performed as long as the worker has access to a computer and connection to the internet in order to bid on the job and then perform it.[13] In the case of Amazon Mechanical Turk, owned and operated by Amazon.com, the site focuses on discrete job units ("human intelligence tasks," or HITs, in the platform's parlance) that are computationally difficult to achieve, such as content screening and moderation. Its website describes its philosophy for prospective workers:

> Amazon Mechanical Turk is based on the idea that there are still many things that human beings can do much more effectively than computers, such as identifying objects in a photo or video, performing data de-duplication, transcribing audio recordings, or researching data details. Traditionally, tasks like this have been accomplished by hiring a large temporary workforce (which is time consuming, expensive, and difficult to scale) or have gone undone.[14]

Microlabor sites represent the most disconnected and disjointed of all the arrangements under which content moderators labor. Additionally, accountability to the worker—for the job tasks, work environment, rate of pay, and so on—is the lowest of all the forms described here. Under the microlabor arrangement, workers can be the most globally dispersed and isolated of all content moderation workers. Their tasks are broken out to their smallest component parts, such that one view of one image may constitute one job, with payment being as low as one cent (U.S. $0.01) for applying a commercial content moderation decision to that image.[15] Fundamentally precarious, workers have no official status with any company, receive no salary or hourly remuneration for their work and no benefits, and are incentivized to do as many tasks as possible to accumulate payment.[16] It is, in effect, digital piecework as a form of gig work, which has been written about extensively by

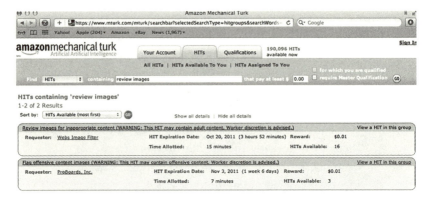

Commercial content moderation work can be found on microlabor task sites such as Amazon Mechanical Turk. In this case, from October 2011, the assignments shown offer a caveat, "Worker discretion is advised." The tasks are viewing and making decisions about potentially "offensive" material or images that "may contain adult content" for a "reward," or payment, of one cent each.

scholars like Lily Irani, Ayhan Aytes, Six Silberman, and Jamie Woodcock, among others.[17]

During the course of my research, I found that companies requiring content moderation services customarily develop hybrid strategies to engage workers through dimensions of the above taxonomy and across numerous labor sites worldwide. They may, for example, maintain a suite of in-house contract workers at the company headquarters who are retained and paid by an outsourcing firm. The in-house team may, in turn, collaborate with teams working at call centers elsewhere in the world, such as in Manila or Gurgaon, who respond to a subset of cases requiring review. A company may hire a boutique firm to manage all aspects of its social media brand identity, including review content uploaded by its users, or it may turn, instead, to microlabor sites like Upwork or Amazon Mechanical Turk to deal with the overwhelming inflow of user-generated content they receive, on a piece-by-piece basis. The largest firms may employ any or all of these techniques and forms of labor to meet their user-generated content processing needs while carefully watching their bottom line, attending to the massive volume of material requiring review, and attempting to reduce both the labor and technology costs associated with content moderation practices whenever possible.

The accuracy of my findings about the hybridity of techniques that platforms deploy to engage workers was underscored when I began interviewing U.S.-based commercial content moderation workers. One research participant who worked as an in-house moderator at MegaTech in Silicon Valley said, "When our shift ends, the team in India comes online." When I asked him if the workers were MegaTech employees, as he saw himself, or contractors, he replied, "Contractors." So, while the MegaTech workers in California fell into the "in-house" category as on-site contractors nonetheless paid by a third-party contracting firm, when contrasted with Indian counterparts, the in-house MegaTech mods saw them as distinctly other: squarely in the "call center" designation and unequivocally contractors at a far remove from MegaTech. This is only one example of how such hybrid strategies are employed to meet the demand of 24/7 moderation at massive scale for sites and platforms with a global user base, while reducing costs for the firms that need such moderation coverage and introducing complex layers of labor stratification and reporting structures. Additionally, social media platforms may turn to these strategies because so much of the work necessitates linguistic and cultural competencies present in abundance only in particular regions, so the locations of the third-party companies offering moderation services, and the skills of their workforce, matter greatly and become a competitive selling point for their services in the marketplace.

Whatever the specific arrangements and strategies implemented to get the work of content moderation done, there tend to be shared characteristics at all levels and among all sites of user-generated content moderation and screening. Screening and moderation tasks are customarily performed by contracting with semipermanent or temporary workers in low-wage, low-status environments. Commercial content moderation itself is both a global industry and set of practices. The work is often performed well removed from the site—and often the country or region—for which the content under review originated or was initially destined. Finally, content moderation of user-generated content fits precisely into new forms of technology-dependent knowledge labor envisioned, initially and optimistically, as having the potential for providing a better quality of work and life, a higher standard of living, and more leisure time to the broad strata of workers engaged in it. In contrast to how that labor environment was envisioned, however, commercial content moderation is work that calls for very large labor forces of not particularly high technical skill engaged in repetitive, unpleasant work. As social media firms' quest for workers willing to perform digital piecework proceeds on a global scale, the remuneration for their labor is offered at ever lower rates. In this way, online content moderation and screening may represent a dystopian, technologically enhanced race to the bottom. The location of the Mechanical Turk worker population, for example, has largely shifted to India, and many who "Turk" as a part- or full-time job receive two dollars per hour or less.[18]

In whatever context a worker might find herself performing commercial content moderation tasks, the likelihood is that the work is not a job for which she has trained, prepared, or studied. Before responding to an ad, being recruited or approached by a contracting agency, or being contacted via other, often indirect or circuitous means, most commercial content moderators have never heard of this type of work. Even following their initial job interviews, they may still not fully understand the nature of the work, which, until relatively recently, did not even exist.

A Brief History of Knowledge Labor in the "Post-Industrial Society"

In 1973, against the backdrop of the Cold War, the Vietnam era, and the advances in science and technology that fueled and were stoked by both, sociologist Daniel Bell published his foundational work *The Coming of Post-Industrial Society.* In it, Bell put forth his vision of a socioeconomic paradigm shift so profound as to represent a "change in the social framework of Western society," and specifically in its economic structure, technological capability, and occupational systems.[19] Characteristics of these shifts, according to Bell, included a movement from a commodity, or goods-oriented, economy to one focused on the service sector; the rise of the technical class engaging in specialized, scientific, or other technical work (for example, data analysis, engineering); and the increased importance and predominance of technological innovation. In concert, Bell prophesied, these shifts would result in a service-based, technology-driven economy, and its stock-in-trade would be production and analysis of new knowledge—the desired output in the post-industrial society and a key component of the socioeconomic arrangements to come.

These shifts, already under way at the time of Bell's writing and with additional shifts "forecasted" (his preferred term), represented an evolutionary leap from the status quo of the structures in place since the great industrialization of the nineteenth century that had endured throughout most of the twentieth century. In the United States, the twentieth century's sites of production were typically factories producing tangible goods en masse. Organizationally, the factories were often arranged in a vertical hierarchy of management and workers in Taylorist tradition, all of whom were long-term employees, generally working on a manufacturing production line. This type of organization and production is usually described as "Fordist," related to the automobile manufacturer's innovations in assembly line production and other efficiencies in production and labor. Accordingly, Bell's description of and prediction for the post-industrial era concluded that the industrial era's commitment to innovation in routinization, mechanization, and other efficiencies of scientific management practices would be carried forward and enhanced by the forecasted socioeconomic shifts.

The imagined result of these shifts would see workers move out of the factories and into offices, working more efficiently but ostensibly for fewer hours, with an enhanced quality of work life and an increase in leisure time. American society would then surge even further to the fore in industries of the future that would be based not on tangible goods manufacturing but rather on scientific and technological innovation. As knowledge production would increasingly become the most important output of workers, the movement from an industrial society, based on mass production of tangible goods, to a post-industrial society, based on the production and, thereby, the commodification of information, would increase.

Indeed, from the 1970s through the mid- to late 1980s, many (but not all) of Bell's predictions had come true: mass production of goods had declined in the United States, while new sectors of innovation in science and technology experienced unprecedented growth. Silicon Valley, for example, experienced its first major period of prominence during this time. By 1976, future tech entrepreneur Marc Porat began his influential dissertation by asserting, "We are now an information economy. Over half our wages and nearly half of our GNP [gross national product] originate with the production, processing and distribution of goods and services," and by as early as 1967, "over half of all labor income [was] earned by workers whose tasks [were] predominantly informational."[20]

Meanwhile, other scholars began to deepen critical analyses of contemporary socioeconomic organization and information and communication technology (ICT) development, many critiquing Bell's largely optimistic view.[21] Sociologist Manuel Castells developed his theory of a "network society," an information-driven economy characterized by the compression of time and space into a "space of flows" and organization and labor practices reconstituted into flexible, reconfigurable, and dynamic structures that more closely resemble interconnected nodes than did the top-down hierarchies of the factories and plants of the industrial era.[22] Such organization, enhanced by the data-driven computational power of global digital connectivity, transcended geospatial boundaries into global networking arrangements and was no longer limited to a traditional workday. Instead, it could function across time zones and around the clock.

Yet this new networked configuration of the post-industrial society did not benefit all. On the contrary, the very characteristics that made it so appealing to some served to reinforce social inequities experienced by many, and to create new ones, too, particularly in arrangements that seemed to benefit the private sector at the expense of the public sphere. Castells, for example, critiqued the post-industrial network society on this basis, cautioning against the new inequities that arose from the geospatial reconfigurations produced by compressed time and space. He described this as a "Fourth World," a new space of interconnected locales around the world whose commonality and connection was predicated not on geographic proximity or a historic trajectory of underdevelopment (due to colonization and its resource extraction, for example, as was the case for many so-called Third World countries), but due to their shared exclusion from the network society.[23] Concern about the exclusion of people from the globally networked world culminated in the identification of the "digital divide" phenomenon in the United States, with an influential study by the National Telecommunications and Information Administration in 1995.[24] Research regarding the nature and character of the informational divide continued throughout the 1990s and into the 2000s, with efforts being made in economically diverse areas of the world to mitigate its damaging effects.[25] Political economists of communication such as Herbert Schiller and Dan Schiller proposed that the "digital divide" was simply an expression of a larger socioeconomic divide: capitalism's schisms as perpetuated by the intertwined lack of access to information and computer technology and a stranglehold by a relative few large corporations over their control.[26]

Indeed, the characteristics of the world economy, too, had begun to significantly shift at the same time as the changes described by Bell, Castells, and others took hold. Markets moved across traditional state and geographic borders in a great global expansion. Because financial information and transactions could more swiftly traverse the globe, respond to changes in markets on a worldwide scale, and be analyzed and reconfigured in increasingly complex, machine-aided ways, governments in major Western countries such as the United States and the United Kingdom increasingly relied on erstwhile fringe economic policies of supply-side economics to advocate and gain a reduction in regulatory and other barriers to market entry and expansion, and the data- and information-driven financial service sector experienced large-scale growth in such areas as investment banking, debt servicing and lending, and speculation.[27]

These sectors made great gains throughout the past forty years, and relied heavily on the features of post-industrial and network society configurations to realize their gains. Yet these sectors' trade in intangible goods and the riches made in that trade were hardly distributed equally; rather, they benefited only a very few, and in very few places around the globe. The digitization of financial markets, in particular, has resulted in what legal scholar Frank Pasquale describes as "the black box society," with its inner workings remaining impenetrable to most and thus increasingly impervious to regulation.[28] These same digital markets have also proved extremely fragile and vulnerable to manipulation, particularly in the past few years, which have seen entire stock markets and other intangible "financial products" greatly lose value or collapse altogether.

The New Nature of Work: Knowledge Labor in the Digital Era

The reorganization of labor into new forms of flexible, distributed global practices has been one of the primary characteristics of the post-industrial/network/knowledge society era since it was first theorized and noted—heralded, by some, as potential freedom from the assembly floor and critiqued by others as perhaps different from, but no better than, past arrangements.[29] These reorganizations are predicated on features such as the global flow of networked information, the proliferation of a distributed workplace organizational model, and an emphasis on immaterial analytical forms of labor.

Yet in some cases, the status and conditions for labor in the post-industrial era may, in fact, be even worse than in the past. Due to the acceleration and compression of time and space, and the global reach of networks that connect labor markets with workers, there has been in many sectors a redistribution of work to its smallest reducible parts and to the lowest possible bids for that work on the world marketplace, as we have seen in the case of Amazon Mechanical Turk's HITs: so-called microtasks and other forms of app-driven gig labor that scholars have demonstrated have deeply racialized and gender-based characteristics of exploitation.[30] In most cases, these functions, and their concomitant exploitative characteristics, are technologically enhanced by computerization and digitization of that work. What, then, does knowledge labor, and labor under post-industrialism, look like?

Among the many insights offered in his book focused on the post-industrial workplace organization of Indian computer programmers, *Virtual Migration,* A. Aneesh provides the following description: "Dominating forms of labor are concerned less and less with manipulating and altering physical objects; rather, programming allows what is in effect a liquefaction of labor, by converting different forms of work . . . into code that can flow online [so that] . . . in a marriage of code and capital, labor increasingly moves in [a] code-based transnational space."[31] Theorist Tiziana Terranova underscores the shift from the production of discrete material goods to a paradigm of networked knowledge work that "is about the extraction of value out of continuous, updateable work, and . . . is extremely labor intensive. It is not enough to produce a good Web site, you need to update it continuously to maintain interest in it and fight off obsolescence. Furthermore, you need updateable equipment (the general intellect is always an assemblage of humans and their machines), in its turn propelled by the intense collective labor of programmers, designers, and workers."[32] The work characteristic of this new epoch is therefore cyclical, symbiotic, and self-perpetuating. Further, as Terranova articulates, a fundamental shift has occurred from the industrial to the post-industrial age whereby the material fabrication of machines supports knowledge labor as the product, rather than knowledge being used in the service of building of machines for the manufacturing of physical objects or other products. Likewise, entire secondary immaterial industries and practices, such as commercial content moderation, have developed in support of that knowledge-labor product. Labor forces from around the globe have been drafted to fulfill this new work need.

Other phenomena have arisen, too, out of the digitization of work practices and the primacy of culture-making knowledge labor, such as the rise of play or leisure activities that actually constitute work and, in many cases, may be performed without traditional remuneration to the worker (for example, editing entries in Wikipedia, quality-assurance testing for games, user-tagging, and other crowd-sourced activities), and the tendency for more and more knowledge work to resemble, or be made to resemble, activities of leisure or play.[33] In some cases, this could include more historical examples of online moderation, or contemporary examples that follow those models, such as volunteer-driven community moderation on sites like Reddit.

Critical digital media scholar Christian Fuchs offers a further analysis of knowledge work and workers that reveals nuance and stratification between "direct" and "indirect" workers. According to Fuchs, "Direct knowledge workers (either employed as wage labour in firms or outsourced, self-employed labour)... produce knowledge goods and services that are sold as commodities on the market (e.g., software, data, statistics, expertise, consultancy, advertisements, media content, films, music, etc.) and indirect knowledge workers ... produce and reproduce the social conditions of the existence of capital and wage labour such as education, social relationships, affects, communication, sex, housework, common knowledge in everyday life, natural resources, nurture, care, etc."[34] This division maps, in many cases, to differences in socioeconomic valuations of that work, as demonstrated by wage and status differentiation. Fuchs views immaterial knowledge work, whether performed through direct or indirect production, as a fundamental characteristic of globalized capitalism, describing the labor as what "produces and distributes information, communication, social relationships, affects, and information and communication technologies."[35]

Commercial content moderation of user-generated content in social media may fit within the bifurcation of knowledge labor as direct or indirect, as described by Fuchs. Or perhaps it constitutes a third, hybrid form of immaterial knowledge labor. This type of labor straddles or bridges the two, requiring specialized cultural, social, and linguistic capital normally associated with direct production of knowledge commodities, for workers to make their judgments based on rules, social norms, and taste (characteristics that seem to fall into the "direct" category), and yet does not produce categorically new knowledge, goods, or services. Rather, commercial content moderation is an act of gatekeeping and curation; simply, albeit importantly, passing along material created by others—a function of replication that would fall into practices labeled by Fuchs as "indirect." Content moderation labor is, in this way, an act of information processing, appraisal, assessment, and evaluation with similarities to other labor practices reliant upon such skills but seldom recognized as such or considered in the same echelon as work requiring expertise.

These theoretical frameworks for knowledge labor underscore many of the greatest shifts away from past labor practices and paradigms, and into both a product of and an actor in the new socioeconomic configurations of the knowledge-based network society. Yet labor in the knowledge economy does not represent a complete rupture from practices of the previous era; rather, it retains key elements from the industrial age that are sustained and enhanced by network-enabled and -enabling technologies and practices. Ursula Huws, for example, notes the following about traditional call centers (a comparable site for low-status immaterial labor): "In many ways, they fit the model 'post-industrial' workplaces: the work is white-collar, requiring considerable amounts of knowledge to perform; it relies crucially on information and communications technology. . . . Yet it exhibits many of the features commonly supposed to epitomise 'industrial' Fordist production, including Taylorist management and a work-pace determined by machines and their programmes."[36]

According to definitions developed by these and other theorists, commercial content moderation workers fit the description of knowledge workers, an artifact of the technologies of the digital network economy, although their labor differs from the high-status, high-wage, creative-class knowledge workers of the late 1990s and early 2000s.[37] Digital knowledge work represents a clear shift away from the agricultural manual labor and manufacturing and industrial production that characterized much of American economic and labor activity until the late twentieth century. Knowledge labor relies instead on a worker's cultural capital and ability to engage with information and communication technology. Increasingly, it relies, too, on locations other than those of the content-hosting entities providing large, cheap pools of laborers (that is, traditional "outsourcing"), culturally and linguistically fluent in Western culture and in American English, who can be digitally networked anywhere in the world, as is the case with the employees of Caleris, the midwestern U.S. call center profiled in the *New York Times* article that first caught my eye.

The Globalized Knowledge Workforce: "Outsourcing" in Rhetoric and Practice

Knowledge labor is not the only kind of work that has sprung up in the digital era. On the contrary, the ICT-reliant network economies are also highly dependent on a great deal of heavy industry and manufacturing to meet their equipment and infrastructure needs. Yet such industrial production is frequently located, through processes and structures of globalization, around the world (typically in the Global South) in such a way to best take advantage of lenient and permissive environmental and labor laws and practices, location of natural resource extraction, and cheaper labor, while simultaneously rendering that production invisible to the socioeconomically elite of the world.[38]

Such arrangements allow the post-industrial era to retain the mythology of its name, an era that, in the West, imagines an evolution beyond the need for coal-belching factories of the nineteenth century or the mind-numbing rote tasks of the twentieth-century assembly line, while engaging in equally environmentally damaging manufacturing activities. Silicon Valley–based labor activist Raj Jayadev has commented on this peculiar collective myopia, saying: "A profound characteristic the popular psyche has accepted about the Information Age is the presumption that technology is produced by some sort of divine intervention so advanced that it requires no actual assembly or manufacturing, the very same features our predecessors in the Industrial Era found so essential. Yet every computer, printer, and technological wizardry in-between bought at the local Radio Shack is birthed in what is usually a very inglorious assembly line production site."[39] This myopia extends, too, to the end of life of these products, frequently hidden from Western consumers via disposal at electronics waste sites in China, the Philippines, India, Ghana, and elsewhere in the Global South.[40]

Likewise, human intervention and immaterial labor is indeed a key, and yet equally cloaked, part of the production chain in sites that rely on user-generated uploaded content requiring screening. Commercial content moderators serve an integral role in making decisions that affect the outcome of what content will be made available on a destination site. The content screeners also view large amounts of material that never makes it long-term to the site or platform it was intended for, as they deem it unfit based on site guidelines, legal prohibition, or matters of taste—their labor literally remaining unseen to anyone who visits the site.

In many cases, great geospatial reconfigurations have taken place to facilitate this hidden manufacturing, the material and immaterial labor underpinning the knowledge economy, as Aihwa Ong, David Harvey, Dan Schiller, and others have demonstrated. These reconfigurations frequently take the form of "special industrial zones" or "special economic zones," particularly in East Asia, where terms are favorable for transnational corporations to base major manufacturing operations, or for local corporations working on contract to such international concerns.[41] The countries that host them and the companies that take advantage of them treat these zones as having different terms of governance than traditional sovereign nation-states. As such, these zones can attract transnational business interests by offering tax exemptions and other sweetheart economic terms that may also include relaxed labor laws or other incentives that leave workers and other citizens at a deficit.

In this sense, the phenomenon of outsourcing might mean something more complex than simply shifting worksites from one nation-state or geographic location to another. In China, for example, its own internal migration of 150 million workers from primarily rural areas to the manufacturing centers concentrated in its special industrial zones is greater than the transnational migration throughout the rest of the world combined.[42] In this way, post-industrial labor configurations have troubled notions of nation-states, border crossing, migration, race, and identity. Highly skilled and well-educated workers from the Global South nevertheless find themselves forced to go abroad for employment, such as the Indian programmers in Berlin profiled in Sareeta Amrute's *Encoding Race, Encoding Class*—racialized, largely segregated from local German communities and their permission to reside in the country tied precariously to their status as temporary knowledge workers.[43] Meanwhile, Western workers find themselves "outsourced" in their own countries of origin, and compared directly to as well as competing directly with counterparts they likely consider a racialized Other halfway around the globe.

Consider the case of the Iowa-based Caleris, where midwestern values were what was on sale. In 2010, Caleris was a call center company offering a suite of business process outsourcing services to potential clients, including content moderation of material uploaded by users. Headquartered in West Ames, Iowa, its worksites at the time were located in several rural, formerly largely agricultural areas of the state. The catchphrase of the business touted its location and the specialized cultural sensibility of its White, as depicted on its website, midwestern American workers through its xenophobia-tinged slogan, "Outsource to Iowa—not India." This phrase was coupled with images featuring bucolic cornfields and iconic red barns and silos invoking Iowa's rich agricultural history, serving as both enticement and reassurance to would-be customers about the cultural orientation, economic status, and political context of the company and its employees. The veracity of the scene was not in question on the Caleris site, but such family farms had by that point mostly given way to large-scale corporate agribusiness throughout the state. Nearby Ames, Iowa, was the site of the Farm Aid benefit concert in 1993, designed to raise awareness and money for family farmers subject to foreclosure.[44] Perhaps just one or two generations ago, the Caleris employees of rural Iowa would have been laboring in fields of the kind invoked through the imagery on its splash screen.

By 2010, Caleris employees at its four call centers in formerly agrarian Iowa existed in a space of outsourcing, competing in a global marketplace in which its cultural capital was invoked as a means to give the company an edge. Indeed, Caleris co-founder Sheldon Ohringer noted in a corporate profile that the low cost of labor and of living in rural Iowa, coupled with a perceived "lack of regional accents" and an intangible set of values on the part of the Iowa-based employees, made the company's commercial content moderation services highly appealing to potential clients. "Iowa, often viewed as the

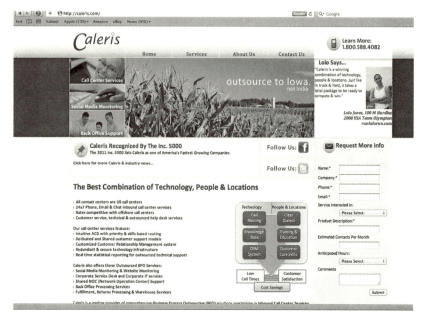

From 2010 to at least 2013, the Caleris home page highlighted its
location in Iowa, "not India," as a selling point for its contract
commercial content moderation and call center services. Caleris
went on to change its tagline to "Premium customer support from
America's heartland" before the firm rebranded as Aureon in 2016.

heart of midwestern values, has served as the perfect place to
draw talented and hard-working individuals whose value systems tend to align with America's view of what is appropriate
when it comes to user-generated content," Ohringer said in a
press release, favorably comparing his employees with those of
direct competitors to his business in countries such as India.[45]

   Geospatial, economic, and political reconfigurations of
intra- and international outsourcing and direct competition
across the globe have been brought to bear in the context of
knowledge work and, specifically, in online commercial content

moderation. Although it has only one-tenth the population of India, the Philippines has now surpassed that country in terms of the actual number of workers in call centers—frequently the site of moderation of user-generated content for social media companies headquartered on the other side of the globe.[46]

Many of these global call center firms solicit for online content moderation clients in Western markets and in English. MicroSourcing, for example, based in the Philippines, appeals to a primarily U.S.-based audience with its reference to and rather positive spin on the Philippines' long history of colonization and cultural domination from the West, specifically and most recently by the United States. On its website, the company touts its employees' excellent command of English and their immersion in Western popular culture ("thanks to their excellent English writing and communication skills . . . and their understanding of Western slang and figures of speech") as a selling point for their services, available on a 24/7/365 basis. Elsewhere on the site, MicroSourcing offers a "Virtual Captives" service for firms wishing to develop and rapidly deploy an offshore team.[47]

The practice of user-generated content moderation at companies like Caleris and MicroSourcing, both of which are call-center-style business process outsourcing firms, poses profound questions about the nature of digital and knowledge labor in the post-industrial era, the nature of the commercialized internet, and the phenomenon of globalization and the socioeconomic and political structures that drive it. Caleris's own slogan, for example, "Outsource to Iowa, not India," identifies the contracted labor it undertakes as a form of outsourcing, suggesting the character and nature of the labor performed—contractual, piecework, precarious, networkable, and so on—as a key shared characteristic with other firms engaged in these

Filipinos have excellent language skills, understand Western slang, and have a great eye for detail, making them perfectly suited for content moderation work.

MicroSourcing, a multi-service business process outsourcing firm based in the Philippines, touts its employees' excellent command of English and their cultural immersion in Western popular culture as a selling point for their content moderation services. The webpage asserts that Filipino people possess innate qualities making them particularly adept at supplying moderation services for North American clientele, including a "great eye for detail."

practices locally. And although it seeks to differentiate itself from India with this slogan, the effect is a rhetorical closing of distance that puts Iowa closer to India in terms of labor pool than a neighboring midwestern American state such as Illinois, Wisconsin, or Nebraska. Those do not register in proximity to Iowa in the map of the world that Caleris has redrawn.

For Caleris, even though the worksites and workers remain inside the geographic boundaries of the United States, the company itself sees the service it provides to U.S. companies as one of outsourcing. Therefore, outsourcing is not just a geographic concept denoted by physical-world spatial characteristics or constraints, but something else: a set of labor processes and configurations, and a designation of an available labor pool, as opposed to simply location. It is a type of work, a wage level, a class of workers whose peripheralization is enabled and enhanced by digitization and the internet's "space of flows"—its cleavage with constraints of chronological time and geophysical space, wherever in the world they may be.[48]

At the same time, both the rhetoric and the practice of outsourcing rely on a transnational bridging of low-wage, low-status, and contractual labor. Under this logic it therefore becomes reasonable for a company such as Caleris to first identify its direct competition as not another midwestern state with similar socioeconomic, political, and cultural characteristics, but India—and to then differentiate itself from India, the Other, by selling its services on the basis of Caleris's cultural intangibles that are as ostensibly White, rural, and American as the red barn and midwestern farm depicted on its home page.

Given the financial, public relations, and political implications and impact a viral video or other highly circulated, highly viewed content can have, the tasks performed by these workers are far from inconsequential. What can be stated unequivocally is that human intervention and immaterial labor are indeed a key, and yet obfuscated, part of the production chain in online sites that rely upon user-generated uploaded content to populate and draw in their producers/users/consumers. Content moderators, whose labor and even mere existence are so frequently hidden from view, nevertheless serve an integral role in making decisions that affect the outcome of what content will be made available on a destination site. While the moderators' work may not be as physically demanding or dangerous as that of those workers whose labor goes into IT hardware manufacturing, it indeed is often disregarded, unmentioned, or unacknowledged—and has its own potential for psychological damage, in terms of the nature of the material to which the moderators may be exposed.

Digital Piecework at Facebook

Against the backdrop of a much publicized and, ultimately, troubled initial public offering, Facebook made a smaller splash in the news in 2012, when facts about its user-generated content moderation practices came to light via the online news and entertainment website Gawker. Several digital pieceworkers performing user-generated content screening through a micro-labor site contacted Gawker staff journalist Adrian Chen. The workers, who reviewed user-generated content for oDesk (now Upwork) on behalf of Facebook, provided Chen with leaked internal oDesk documents describing Facebook's content screening standards and practices that highlighted disturbing aspects of what the workers were required to see.

Chen's subsequent story, "Inside Facebook's Outsourced Anti-Porn and Gore Brigade, Where 'Camel Toes' Are More Offensive Than Crushed Heads," was remarkable in a number of ways: first, he wrote about real-world examples shared with him by the workers, most of whom were no longer working for Facebook via oDesk as digital pieceworkers, and many of whom were located outside the United States (primarily in the Global South).[49] The workers' accounts gave concrete examples of the kinds of trauma-inducing material they were exposed to while being paid digital piecework–level wages that seemed disproportionate to the psychological hazards of their work.

Second, the workers provided Chen with internal documents from oDesk used for training and quality control by the content screeners. This type of material is generally not available for public view and is considered proprietary information by both the companies providing commercial content moderation and those that contract for moderation of user-generated content destined for their sites. But protecting this information as trade secrets obscures other issues, allowing a company to legally maintain ambiguity about its screening and censoring practices, and giving in to a larger propensity toward a logic of opacity that "can lead users to have wildly different interpretations of the user experience on the same site . . . [and that] renders the machinery of content moderation opaque."[50] More general "user guideline"–style statements give plenty of room in which to operate when making subjective content screening decisions. Chen's piece also pointed out the strange hierarchy of user-generated material as subject to social media firms' particular internal logic, and oDesk's protocols for adjudicating it by the screeners.

While other media seized on the sensationalistic aspects of the story, just below the surface were even more compelling facts.[51] For example, the internal oDesk documents provide a great deal of insight into the kinds of material that the low-paid contract laborers were expected to see.[52] Images and videos of animal abuse and mutilation, child abuse (physical and sexual), gore, disturbing racist imagery, and so on occurred so often that there were specialized protocols devoted to handling them—keeping them from making it to the site if they were not yet there, and removing them if they were.

Not long after the news about Facebook moderation via oDesk broke, Facebook released a confusing infographic ostensibly designed to shed light on the cryptic route that reported content takes through the company's circuit of screening. According to the company, content flagged as inappropriate, for any one of myriad reasons, makes its way to "staffers in several offices around the world to handle the millions of user reports it receives every week about everything from spam to threats of violence."[53] Reasons cited in the infographic that may result in material being reported include content that is sexually explicit, involves harm to self or others, depicts graphic violence, contains hate speech, and so on.

What was missing, however, from Facebook's infographic and accompanying statement was any suggestion of how much content is routed through this circuit, and how significant a problem routinely addressing inappropriate user-generated content tends to be. Critically lacking was any discussion of the status or the working conditions of the "staffers . . . around the world" who contend with this distressing material as a major function of their job. The leak did confirm that Facebook at least at that time had employed microlabor companies such as oDesk/Upwork, and potentially others, to conduct these moderation and review practices. The workers engage in digital piecework offered on microwork sites and are therefore afforded no protections or benefits whatsoever. Further, their physical and geographical isolation from their co-workers means they cannot support or commiserate with one another about the content they view as a condition of their work, a key coping mechanism for content moderation workers.

In this way, Facebook benefited from the lack of accountability that comes with outsourcing; that is, introducing secondary and tertiary contracting firms into the cycle of production—a fact that is critically absent from the infographic. Workers engaged as moderators through digital piecework sites are isolated, with few (if any) options for connecting—for emotional support as well as for labor organizing—with other workers in similar conditions, and without any real connection to the original worksites from which the content emanates.

Another little-publicized aspect of outsourcing is that, while the microwork sites and the major corporations that engage them may tout the ability to draw on expertise from a global labor marketplace, in practice these temporary work relationships result in lost payroll-tax revenue for countries such as the United States when labor is outsourced from it, and in significant increases in these kinds of labor pools in Greece and Spain, countries devastated by economic crisis and crippling "austerity" measures.[54] Indeed, the worldwide marketplace for digital piecework allows for bargain-basement rates that, by design, drive the value of the labor down to the lowest global bidder. The connection between economic crisis in a region and an increase in the availability of competent labor that is exceedingly cheap cannot be lost in this analysis.

Why Commercial Content Moderation Matters

As a central and mission-critical activity in the workflow of online digital media production, commercial content moderation is little known, frequently low-wage/low-status, and generally outsourced. Content moderation ensures brand protection, adherence to terms-of-use statements, site guidelines, and legal regimes (for example, copyright, law enforcement). It is a key part of the production chain of commercial sites and social media platforms, yet companies often distance themselves from this work and dislike publicity about their moderation practices.

But it also complicates, troubles, and directly contradicts notions of the internet as a free-speech zone. It introduces the existence of human decision-makers unknown to and unseen by the vast majority of end users, who are nevertheless critical in the production chain of social media decision-making. Their invisible presence disrupts comfortable and commonplace notions predicated on the one-to-one relationship of user-to-platform. It paints a disturbing view of an unpleasant work task that the existence of social media and the commercial, regulated internet, in general, necessitate.

Certainly, early theorists of the post-industrial age envisioned the morphing of the industrial twentieth century into
the post-industrial twenty-first century as ripe with possibility
for greater flexibility, mobility, higher-status work, and more
leisure time for American workers, who would shift to using
their analytical and technical acumen developed from their
production abilities and migrate to a knowledge-based economy of high-status, high-wage work. Yet, the vision promul-
gated by Bell and the technological deterministic futurists who
came in his wake has increasingly ceded to a different reality.
Rather than elevating the workers of the world, twenty-first-
century configurations of labor are undergoing a globalized
race to the bottom in search of ever cheaper, faster, and more
human and material resources to compete in the globalized,
24/7 networked marketplace.

Finally, although there has been a great emphasis and
primacy placed on knowledge work under post-industrial social
arrangements, heavy industry and manufacturing of all sorts
are still alive and critically important, even to the knowledge
economy, suggesting a shift rather than supersession. The post-
industrial labor economy has demanded great geospatial
rearrangements and migrations of people, whose "flexibility"
is often synonymous with "instability," "precarity," or "margin-
ality," as scholars like Jack Linchuan Qiu have shown.[55] To
paraphrase Tiziana Terranova, labor under the knowledge
economy may just not be as fun as it has been made out to be.[56]
In order to contend with what is wrong with labor under the
current socioeconomic structures, with the purpose of better-
ing it, we must continue to unveil the realities of labor and
other costs (environmental, for example) of the knowledge and
digital economies, on a global scale and in all strata.[57]

3
Screening in Silicon Valley

I can't imagine anyone who does [this] job and is able to just walk out at the end of their shift and just be done. You dwell on it, whether you want to or not.

—Max Breen

It's factory work, almost. It's doing the same thing over and over.

—Josh Santos

In the fall of 2012, I interviewed Max Breen, a twenty-four-year-old White graduate of a private alternative West Coast liberal arts college, working in his second job in Silicon Valley as a full-time customer service agent in the technology industry and living with his girlfriend and several roommates in San Francisco.[1] Although his previous employment as a commercial content moderator was governed, as is typically the case, by a nondisclosure agreement that ostensibly precluded him from sharing details of his job, Max was eager to talk to me and share his experiences and insights into his work life in his previous role as contractor at MegaTech, a major multinational internet giant.

At the time of our interview, Max had been off the MegaTech gig for a year and was working in another small Silicon Valley startup after a period of unemployment. At MegaTech, he and his fellow commercial content moderation workers, colloquially known as "admins" when on the job, had all been in-house contractors, and each was granted a one-year term of employment, with the potential for one additional year of contract renewal after a mandatory three-month break.

His colleague, Josh Santos, also twenty-four and of Cuban-American descent, was finishing out his own year-long contract at MegaTech. He had been recruited by and was technically working for the contracting firm TCX, but he had spent his past year in-house at MegaTech HQ, where he was in his last week as a moderator when we spoke. Josh had attended the University of California, Berkeley, and had spent the year after graduation in service jobs in southern California before starting his job in commercial content moderation at MegaTech. Twenty-three-year-old Caitlyn Brooks, a White Berkeley grad who had majored in economics, was one of the newest members of MegaTech's commercial content moderation contractor team. Only three months into her job at the time of our conversation, Caitlyn said the position with MegaTech was the first full-time employment she had ever had. I spoke to all of them over a period of one month.

Working in-house and on site at MegaTech's sprawling Silicon Valley corporate campus, on a small team, Max, Josh, and Caitlyn spent their days (and some nights and weekends) in the relative comfort and socially upwardly-mobile environment of the iconic successful twenty-first-century tech firm. All of them came to their commercial content moderation job with little experience in tech, and with no prior knowledge of the existence of or need for commercial content moderation.

While all commercial content moderation contractors for MegaTech were required to be college graduates, typically from elite schools with name recognition, they came not from the science, technology, engineering, and medicine (STEM) backgrounds typical of Silicon Valley's engineering and product development teams, but instead from a variety of liberal arts and humanities fields. To them, the chance to work in the new media economy of northern California's tech industry was alluring and loaded with promise, and to have obtained full-time post-graduation employment after the downturn of the larger American economy in 2008 left them feeling lucky and ahead of their peers.

Commercial content moderation jobs seemed, then, to offer a way up and out of their more obvious employment choices in the service-based economy, where even positions in restaurants and food preparation were hard to come by for many new college graduates. But the experiences of the workers I spoke to at MegaTech often gave them pause and occasion to reflect on the nature of their work and on the social-media-fueled economy, in spite of what they were likely to characterize as luck or good fortune in terms of being employed at all. This chapter documents their experiences—all at different points in their stints as commercial content moderators at MegaTech—in detail and, whenever possible, in their own words.

Talkative and gregarious, Max Breen connected with me one late evening over Skype. Of the three workers, Max had a particularly acute awareness of the value of the fundamental role and services he and his colleagues provided, both when the moderation was on behalf of MegaTech's own social media properties and for those of the companies for which commercial content moderation services had been contracted. He eagerly described to me his background and how he came to join the admin team at MegaTech.

> I wasn't actually technically contracted by Mega-Tech itself; I was a contractor working for this contracting company called TCX—I forget what the initials actually stand for. But they were one of three companies that hired contractors for this position at MegaTech ... anyway they called me up and said you know, we're looking for people like you who have recently graduated and may not have a ton of work experience but have a bachelor's degree from a good university and are interested in this kind of work. It was my only job interview of any place I applied for, including being like a cash register jockey at a pizza place, so I kinda jumped on it. Had one in-person interview with some of the people at MegaTech, and that was that. It was a pretty easy hiring process. They were looking for people that came from fairly rigorous schools to show they had that kind of work ethic. . . . I know there were a bunch of people from Cal, there were a couple of people from Duke, so they were all kind of big-name or otherwise well-known rigorous schools. I think that was the gist. I was a history major, there were a bunch of English majors. No real math or science people—they all got like engineering-style jobs. Mostly humanities people.

Before he was hired by TCX, Max had never given any thought to the practice of commercial content moderation, or to the people that might do it. In his early conversations with TCX, they did not disclose complete details to him about the nature of the job. He reported:

> TCX was rather vague about what exactly I would be doing for them. They said I would be handling user reports, but I wasn't sure that was going to be flag videos or copywriting, or what. During my interview and before the interview there was a written test thing, and there they were very clear that like, you are going to see disturbing content, this is not necessarily the easiest job, emotionally speaking. So I think they made it very clear before I started, during the written part of the interview, and communication between my offer and start date that it was serious material—not something that you can just kind of bullshit your way through, like, you have to be very prepared for this.

When Josh Santos came to MegaTech as a contractor, he had a slight edge in knowledge about the position and about commercial content moderation work in general, because his friend, Max, had encouraged him to apply. But he was nevertheless still vague on the details. Like Max, he was attracted to the work because of the prestige of working for a firm with the reputation and name recognition that MegaTech possessed. Also like Max, Josh was a recent college grad facing a daunting and difficult economic environment where job prospects and future opportunities were unsure. He explained:

I had heard about this job, and my friend Max had it earlier, like the year before. And he recommended me and said, "You won't even have to interview, you are going to get this job." And I was like, "Oh, that sounds great!" Cause at the time it was impossible to find any type of work. So, I interviewed for it and I didn't really know what I was getting myself into. I don't mean that in a negative connotation, just mean I had no idea what the job really entailed. Well, it's MegaTech, that's going to look good on my résumé and it's going to get me out of southern Orange County, so I'll take it.

After graduating in 2011, Caitlyn Brooks had struggled to find her place, post-college, and to put value on her education, despite it having been at the world-renowned University of California, Berkeley. She stated:

Well, I'm originally from LA. And, more specifically, West Hollywood, which no one my age is from because there's no kids. And then I came up to Berkeley for school and it was pretty different. Just like the culture is really different, the weather and climate's just not as nice here. But then I made all my friends here and after I graduated I went back home for like almost a year, but I couldn't, it was just hard to find jobs there and like the types of jobs are different. I feel like my diploma wasn't worth as much down there? I don't know. It's kind of weird but it's just a lot easier to find something up here. And I couldn't, I was just bored and stuff and all my friends were just up here so I moved back to like Berkeley. And my second day back I had an interview with MegaTech and I was like, "Wow, that was really fast." And that week I found out I got the job and I was like, "Wow! Things are working out!"

While Josh's entrée into commercial content moderation came directly from his connection with a current employee, Caitlyn found her way to the work through a slightly more circuitous route. She had been using social networking for her post-college job search; in particular, non-STEM graduates from prestigious Berkeley were being targeted for commercial content moderation jobs by the contracting companies hired by MegaTech to staff their in-house commercial content moderation team. Like both Josh and Max, her knowledge about the position and even the function of or need for commercial content moderation was very limited prior to starting the job, but the allure of MegaTech was strong for her, too. And despite what may have constituted a warning from the contracting firm and the MegaTech representatives about the nature of the job, Caitlyn still had very little understanding of the particulars before starting. She reported:

> I found out through, it was in a LinkedIn group for Cal alumni, because I went to Berkeley, and they were looking for people for the MegaTech enforcement team and I didn't really know what that meant at all. And I was like, "It sounds like the police or something." And I was like, "Yeah, it's Mega-Tech, sounds cool." So I just sent my résumé to the girl and they sent me a quiz to take that seems really MegaTech–like. The quiz was based on, it was

like stuff you'd be doing during the job. And then I interviewed in person with a few different people and it was like, they were really cool and relaxed, and they mentioned that you'd see really graphic stuff and that you'd have weird hours. But during the interview you don't really know what that means until you are actually doing the job. Which I found out later was a bigger deal. Once I was there.

She continued, discussing her training for the job, which belied a certain early-stage naiveté about the need for commercial content moderation that her more seasoned counterparts no longer shared and that she, too, had just begun to shed during her tenure at MegaTech. She quickly discovered that even having been a long-term MegaTech user before taking the job would not adequately prepare her for the kind of content she would be responsible for reviewing and, likely, removing: "I mean, I knew it was looking at videos and stuff but even when we're doing the [job training] quiz, they asked us to look for just content that we would have to take down. But I've never been in the mindset of looking for stuff [as just a Mega-Tech user] that obviously shouldn't be up there, and I never really found that weird stuff [on my own]. I usually watch music videos or something."

Caitlyn had never sought out such content as a MegaTech user and was not even aware of its existence. Yet just a short time into her role as a MegaTech admin, she began to connect the material she was responsible for reviewing to larger issues taking place around the globe: "Not like people getting executed or something. I didn't think of all that. And just how all the stuff that's happening in other parts of the world goes to us first. Or it seems like it. Like everyone has a camera now so everyone's putting their really weird stuff and we're the ones seeing it. And I just didn't anticipate that."

Despite the difficult nature of the work she was doing, at the time we spoke, Caitlyn's overarching sentiment toward MegaTech was one of gratitude. As a non-STEM college graduate, albeit from a prestigious university, she still had little sense of what she wanted for her future, and the bigger-picture economic situation for people of her age and experience had led her to feel that her employment options upon graduation would be limited, at best.

For that reason, she was happy to have her job, despite any shortcomings it might have held. Indeed, the economic stress of a poor entry-level job market was a refrain in the interviews with all three of the young MegaTech commercial content moderation workers with whom I spoke, and it directly dictated their actions in terms of the employment decisions they made. Caitlyn summed it up concisely: "I'm just glad to have a job. I don't really . . . I can't complain because it's not like we're . . . we could be doing something so much worse. Like it's still at MegaTech, it's pretty cushy."

No Climbing Wall, No Sushi, No Insurance: MegaTech Contractor Culture

To be a limited-term employee is to be precarious, living in a state of employment-related uncertainty and insecurity. It was therefore no surprise that all three MegaTech commercial content moderation contractors expressed a desire for a permanent job at MegaTech. Indeed, it was the MegaTech name and reputation and all it portended for their imagined futures that drew them in initially. But reality painted a different picture. The terms of their employment were: one year of contract labor via one of several third-party firms, to be undertaken at MegaTech's main campus.

Unlike workers employed directly by MegaTech, they received an hourly wage, rather than salaries, and were barred from many of the benefits of full-time employment. As part of the terms of their employment as designated by MegaTech itself and subsequently meted out by its contractor partners, contractor admins like Max, Josh, and Caitlyn would work for one year and, at the end of that period, would be required to either find new employment or take a mandatory three-month leave. After the three months, they would be eligible to extend their contracts for one more year, but after that, employment in the commercial content moderation group would be terminated.

Although the members of the moderation team I talked to hoped that such expertise, experience, and knowledge of the MegaTech corporate culture and products might lead to full-time, permanent employment elsewhere in the company, Max knew of only one or two former team members for whom such a transition ever materialized. He linked this to a larger-scale culture of ostracism and pervasive undervaluing of contractors at MegaTech, in general, and of the professional content screeners particularly. This treating of commercial content moderation contractors at MegaTech as invisible and disposable—despite the critical importance of their work—manifested itself in ways large and small, from the social opportunities to the material conditions of the work the team performed. As Max Breen reported, "[The commercial content moderation contractors were] vastly underappreciated. We made good money. Or at least absolutely for a first job out of college when most of my friends are baristas or cashiers or whatever. Good money. But you are still contractors, not a full employee. You don't get to go to the Christmas party or whatever. But actually, my manager was super rad. She found enough people in the company with plus-ones that they weren't going to use to get us all in."

Max continued, describing the ways that the devaluing of commercial content moderation work at MegaTech meant that the custom-built set of digital tools they used to manage content workflow was woefully inadequate and that the knowledge and experience accumulated by team members was not recognized in other areas of the company.

> [My manager] went out of her way because she realized, too, that we were underappreciated and we didn't have enough engineering support, so our tools were way out of date 'cause they were from years before I started. And they needed to be updated to handle new features of the site and stuff, but we didn't have the engineering bandwidth to do it. So, she understood a lot of the frustration and did her best to mitigate it. But the company itself was vastly under-appreciating. The simplest thing they could have done to make people happier, because obviously you can't make them happier by changing the content because that isn't up to you, you have to review what you get. But make some sort of path to full-time employee. Because, oh my God, we already know all the systems, we know the policies, that should be a no-brainer. Because they were constantly expanding Copyright, Partner Managers, the Security and Policy team, whoever, they were constantly expanding. But the same external hire rules applied to us. We were not considered part of the company.

At the time we talked, Max had been out of his MegaTech commercial content moderation experience for almost a year. As a contractor, he worked at MegaTech for an hourly wage and was barred from some of the more storied facilities and amenities for which Valley tech companies have become notorious, such as climbing walls, on-site haircuts, and free sushi, a fact he joked about at several points in our interviews.

But Max and his team were also shut out from other benefits that MegaTech's full-timers received: namely, health insurance benefits. The lack of health insurance would play a larger role later in our conversations, but it underscored Max's recognition that his team of contract commercial content moderation workers on site at MegaTech lacked status and respect from other workers and managers who were full-time, direct employees of the extremely wealthy firm. This, coupled with what appeared to be a career-ending revolving door in and out of the commercial content moderation group at MegaTech, bothered Max.

> In the time I was there, we had two people go from contractors to full-time. One was something of an anomaly because he was much older than the rest of us. He had a master's, which none of us had, which was a giant step up, and he spoke Arabic, which was a very severe need, and, as far as I understand, was hired with a guarantee to be given a full-time position. So really there was only one guy who went from contract to full-time. That would be the single easiest thing to boost morale and help people feel more a part of the company. And that didn't happen. Even just little things that, while I understand them logically, really contributed to us not

feeling welcome. This is the stupidest thing in retrospect, but there was a rock-climbing wall in the lobby. Rad. We couldn't use it because we weren't on MegaTech's company insurance plan. We were individual contractors and not covered. And admittedly, logically, I understand, we're not covered. We can't do that. But, like, you pass it every day in the lobby and think, "I'm one of ten people in this company of hundreds that can't use that right there." And that's so frustrating.

Josh Santos was frustrated, too, by MegaTech's corporate culture regarding its commercial content moderation workers. Specifically, he resented its demand that all employees, even lower-status, hourly, limited-term contractors, contribute additional uncompensated intellectual labor. He consciously resisted this aspect of MegaTech's workplace culture. This set him apart from his contractor colleagues on the commercial content moderation team, many of whom, he suspected, continued to hold out hope to earn permanent employee status at MegaTech by generating innovations through uncompensated, additional labor for the company outside the bounds of their job descriptions. Josh found the expectation by his non-contractor supervisors a distasteful imposition.

> They give us incentives to do other projects besides our core work, like we have the option to do projects. And a lot of [moderation] admins do take our bosses up on that. "Oh, yeah, I'd love to do other projects." They're trying to kind of get their foot in the door and maybe get a job afterwards. But I'm not really into that because I've seen over and over

again very talented, very bright admins not get
[permanent] work. We've seen admins who have
done just phenomenal work in projects that our
higher ups would never even dream about, and
they've done it and presented it and they've done
it all on their own, and then at the end of their
contract they're like, "Okay, bye." And after seeing
that over and over, I am not going to even bother
doing extra work. I'm going to do, like, what I got
hired for.

Despite his numerous frustrations with aspects of the
contractor versus full-timer corporate culture at MegaTech,
and the low status afforded the commercial content moderation team, Josh had no trouble delineating his reasons for going
after the job in the first place. In fact, Josh, and others like
him, had performed the calculus of weighing the monetary
and other material benefits (as well as those suggested or
imagined, such as a pathway to permanent MegaTech employment, or the pedigree potential offered by having a MegaTech
gig on one's résumé) for whatever damage the job might cause.
He told me: "My last job paid me three times less when I used
to work as a server at a restaurant. And it was like so much
more work for such little, like, just like no, almost minimum
wage. And so to go from that . . . I think we're all very
young. Like no one is coming from another tech job. Most
other people on our team are coming straight out of school
or straight after their shitty college job. This is really like for
most people on the team this is their first real look at a corporate job, or a professional job. So I think a lot of people kind
of stomach what they have to watch just to keep the perks of
the job."

Moderation at MegaTech: Screening at the Factory

At MegaTech, the commercial content moderation function that required the most human intervention—typically, the viewing and reviewing of video content that had been flagged by the platform's own end users as inappropriate—was kept almost exclusively among the in-house contractors making up the admin team and in MegaTech's homebrewed routing and queue system. The contractors in the commercial content moderation department were responsible for reviewing content that had already been uploaded but had been flagged by users for review or violations of community guidelines; other kinds of problematic content, such as material that violated media holders' copyright, was dealt with in an automated fashion and typically never crossed the desks of MegaTech's admins.

What they saw, instead, was content that was flagged for review on other grounds: that it violated MegaTech's own interdiction against violent, sexually explicit, graphic, disgusting, or abusive content. MegaTech received hundreds of hours of uploaded video per minute, so the commercial content moderation objective at the firm was one of putting out fires: to respond to user-filed complaints quickly, efficiently, and according to internal guidelines that, once learned and employed over and over again, became rote.

MegaTech, a publicly traded multinational corporation, had uncommonly good technology and financial resources available to it; accordingly, the firm had both the expertise and financial means to build internal tools that responded to the specific needs of its platform and the moderators dealing with the volumes of user-uploaded video content they solicited. The workers in the commercial content moderation department used a suite of tools that had been developed for them, often with tweaks and adjustments based on their feedback. According to Max Breen:

> Basically, the bulk of my work was: any time you find a video on MegaTech that you [the user] don't like or find objectionable or what have you, there's a little flag button at the bottom of it that will send it through a couple layers of automation [for copyright violations or through pornography-sensitive filters, for example] and if it's not okayed or removed by those automatic functions, it would come to us. The way it would work, we would get the videos in batches of ten. And each video would, thank God, would auto-generate maybe thirty thumbnails, so you wouldn't have to watch the majority of the videos, just the stills. And you'd do a batch of ten, submit, and move on to the next batch. I would do anywhere from about 1,500 to 2,000 videos a day.

MegaTech's internal routing tools relegated content to one of several queues, depending on the type of violation its end users had reported. These queues often differed in a number of key characteristics regarding the type of content they likely contained, a characteristic that was tied to the kind of response time expected from the reviewer on the commercial content moderation team. Max said: "Tier 1 is speed. You want right decisions, but you've got a ton of videos to get through . . . so you'd get a thumbnail in each queue, some you had to watch the videos of, some you didn't. You could always watch the video. That was always an option, it wasn't just the thumbnails. But that was the main way we screened."

Not only was the productivity of the workers tied to their mastery of internal policies and protocols, it depended on their ability to use the internal and proprietary tools designed for the purpose of managing MegaTech's massive amount of uploaded content, as Max described.

> It was, we had this big list of all the queues and the number of videos awaiting review in each queue and you'd just select which you were going to work in. Which was 90 percent of the time Tier 1. And it would just spit you out a batch of ten videos and it would just go full screen for the most part, that would be my whole main monitor. Then I would have stuff on the side. Twitter, a video, whatever. And it would just be one video per screen, and when you were done with that and you'd made your decision you would, it would just flip to the next video. And once you did ten you submitted the batch and it would pull you another batch out of the queue. There were hot keys, but the hot keys really just activated a pull-down menu. By the end I think it took me a second, two seconds, three seconds of video. I just knew all the hot keys so well, it's like touch-typing by that point.

Josh Santos described how, a year after Max's departure from its moderation team, the process at MegaTech had evolved past keeping everything in-house all the time, to include a team of contractors based in India handling some of the most clear-cut cases of policy violations. Content considered the easiest or most straightforward to adjudicate was deemed appropriate for outsourcing to contractors in other parts of the world.

Under this system, a ranking of complexity was developed regarding the content itself and the nature of complaints about it. By Josh's time on the job, the batch processing of video thumbnails had quadrupled, from a screen of ten at a time to forty. Josh said:

> Our tools are very straightforward. I mean we have what's called a queue, and whenever anything is flagged it goes into this queue. Depending on the flag, it gets separated into different things. If a user flags it for pornography it gets sent to our team in India—they handle the pornography mostly. But anything else, like hate speech or violence, something like that, will get sent to us. And then we basically get it in batches, and then we basically, there's no rhyme or reason to it, it's just you might get a violence video followed by three hate speech videos followed by a harassment video followed by two more violence. And then we have a series of hot keys that correspond to our policies. So essentially the way it works out is you get a video, and it's separated into stills, into little thumbs. We get forty little thumbnails, that way we don't have to watch the video we can instantly see "oh, well there's some genitals" or "there's a man's head but he's not connected to it" ... something like that. And we can instantly apply policy. It's extremely streamlined.

To skillfully and adeptly contend with problematic, disturbing, or upsetting user-generated content at scale, Josh's coping mechanisms went beyond mastery of the technological toolset he had available, and into strategies involving his emotional well-being. Namely, he sought to divorce himself from emotional responses in order to be able to process the flagged content at the high volume required. "I mean, there isn't really much to the job description other than you moderate the stuff that's flagged," he said. "If it violates our policies, we take it down. Otherwise we keep it up. And then like everyone tells you it's going to be like a lot of violence, and you're going to see a lot of heinous, just the dearth of humanity, like, just all day. And that's not a far cry from the truth. That is what you see all day. Violence and pornography. And it takes a certain level of apathy to kind of deal with it, I would say."

Caitlyn, the most recent hire of the three, verified the description of the daily work expectations given by both Max and Josh in her comments to me.

> I carpool in the morning and get there at like 8:30 and we have breakfast. And then basically the whole day we're just supposed to do one task and that's looking at the queue and all the videos and just making sure that, we have to keep the queue down to like under an hour [for response time after flagging]. Videos have to be flagged. Like, we're just trying to, how do I say this? We try to make it so that the videos have been looked at within like an hour of being flagged, by us. So, [we are in] our little dashboard thing, and we just look at tons of videos. They're not filtered into different categories, just like maybe by languages. But then that's basically it. We see a lot of violent stuff, porn, and sexual stuff like that . . . harassment, and hate. Like

everything that's been flagged goes in the same place, and spam too. We just look at that throughout the day. And then we take breaks. Because it might be too much or we have lunch, and then we keep doing that.

If microlabor websites such as Upwork and Amazon Mechanical Turk supply work in a form most resembling digital piecework, then in-house, call center, and other similar commercial content moderation screening jobs as described by Caitlyn, Max, and Josh represent the work of the new digital assembly line: rote, repetitive, quota-driven, queue-based, automated tasks relying on mechanization and rationalized management practices and serving up metrics to assess employee productivity and efficiency.

Rather than the creative, self-expressive work that has typically characterized the best depictions of the tech industry, and the subset based around social media, the environment and rote, repetitive, and endless work tasks at MegaTech's moderation team resembled something much more classical in arrangement: the digital factory. Indeed, Josh directly invoked the specter of the factory and assembly line work as an analogy when describing the conditions and expectations of his commercial content moderation job, saying: "It's factory work, almost. It's doing the same thing over and over."

Who Decides? Internal Policy Development and Application at MegaTech

The admins screening content at MegaTech operated under a regime of internal policies developed by a group of full-time employees to whom they reported: the Security and Policy, or SecPol, group. The internal, extremely detailed policies by which the commercial content moderation workers adjudicated content were not available to the public but, rather, were treated as trade secrets to be used internally, and ultimately functioned in the service of brand management for MegaTech. In part, the secrecy was because of the potential of unscrupulous users who might attempt to game the policies by working very close to the line or just far enough over it to keep questionable content posted on the platform. However, revealing commercial content moderation policies would also allow outsiders to breach the secrecy around the nature of the work of the Mega-Tech admins. The type of content that triggered the moderation process to begin would also be made known if the internal policies were publicized, thereby bringing to light a very ugly reality and underside of a platform with a shiny public image of providing entertainment, fun, and access to broadcasting one's self-expression, whatever that might be, from user to platform, and platform to the world. It could also trigger difficult questions about the values undergirding those policies, a fact of which the moderation admins were certainly aware. As Josh told me, "We try to keep a global viewpoint when applying our policies. At least that's what they say. I feel like they really are grounded in American values, because things like nudity, and I mean just like topless nudity, that's fine in many European nations or like anywhere they're fine with topless nudity except like the Middle East and Japan, but here we take those down."

As commercial content moderation workers like Josh pointed out, while MegaTech is a corporation whose very name is analogous to the internet itself and, as such, has a global reach and user base, its policies regarding user-generated content were developed in the specific and rarefied sociocultural context of educated, economically elite, politically libertarian, and racially monochromatic Silicon Valley, USA. The firm's internal policies often reflected the needs of the company for brand protection first, and, symbiotically, as a mechanism for the enactment of a distinctly American libertarian approach to interpretations of concepts such as free speech and information access. Social mores, too, were refracted through a decidedly American and Western cultural lens and tended to favor the perceived sensibilities of white people, for one.

Commercial content moderation workers therefore can be seen as proxies and conduits for all of these complex sets of values and cultural systems favored by the platforms, even when the company's rules clashed with the employee's own values. Max explained:

> We have very, very specific itemized internal policies. The internal policies are not made public because then it becomes very easy to skirt them to essentially the point of breaking them. We had very specific internal policies that we were constantly, we would meet once a week with SecPol to discuss, there was one, blackface is not technically considered hate speech by default. Which always rubbed me the wrong way, so I had probably ten meltdowns about that. When we were having these meetings discussing policy and, to be fair to them, they always listened to me, they never shut me up. They didn't agree, and they never changed the policy, but they always let me have my say, which was surprising. So yeah, we had dozens of pages of the internal policy that we would apply to the videos.

This nebulous language, he went on to explain, "basically gives us wiggle room." At MegaTech, the internal policies on removing content responded to and reflected a number of other dynamics: publicized community guidelines available to all users; content owners' wishes for a takedown of content posted without consent, and a constantly shifting internal relationship to interpretations of the user-facing guidelines that moderators were required to implement. As Josh explained, "Policies are really about the social climate, so if something becomes acceptable socially, then we'll change our policies, but otherwise policies respond to the global social climate. Like, we have, basically our policies are meant to protect certain groups."

Indeed, some groups were treated differently at MegaTech, despite the existence of policies and protocols, because of the nature of their contributions to MegaTech's success. This typically meant a big "partner," a producer of content whose material drove users in large quantities to MegaTech, thereby earning advertising dollars for itself and for the platform. Max described the relationship:

> If you are a good enough user you can enroll in the partner program, and that gives you a cut of that ad revenue. The partners could write directly to SecPol and Legal Support and sometimes we would get a video that was, say, a partner that would normally warrant a strike on their account and removal of the video ... it was a three-strikes-and-you're-banned [rule]. But maybe they're a big-deal partner and we don't want to ban them, so we would send it to SecPol and they would talk to them. I should be clear: they would not leave the partner's videos up. They would tell them to take it down

and they would be a little more specific than our policy page would be about what the specific violation was, but we didn't, as far as I know, we never broke the rules for partners, we might bend them a tiny bit, but there was never any out and out leaving something objectionable up.

Some types of content and behaviors that straddled lines of acceptability on the platform were a constant source of commercial content moderation work at MegaTech. Max described one particular type that got under his skin, and yet was close enough to technically not breaking the letter of the internal MegaTech content policies that they took a lot of work to address and evaluate.

There was a big problem and I would be almost certain it's still a problem, with dare videos. Where it would mostly be early teen girls, sometimes teen boys but not that often, would have MegaTech accounts without their parents knowing, saying "we're bored, give us dares." And creepos would find them and say "show us your feet." Or things that are sexual, but the kids don't understand that they're sexual. And it was really creepy. And this guy, that's what he did, he found those and flagged them for us and we took them down. It was awesome. I mean, I try not to think about the fact that he might have been into that and that's how he could cover his bases if someone ever came asking about why do you watch all these videos. But the fact is we took down thousands and thousands of those videos off that guy's flags.

For Josh, his status as a contractor for MegaTech and not a full-time MegaTech employee had ramifications where internal policy development was concerned. While full-time employees from the higher-status SecPol team and other full-time employees involved in commercial content moderation functions frequently suggested to the contract MegaTech admins that their input was valued in terms of future policy development or changes or tweaks to extant policy, Josh felt that it was simply lip service. Despite the fact that he was an expert on both the kind of objectionable content seen in the queues, and MegaTech's own internal policy, he was frustrated by a sense of powerlessness to effect real change. The commercial content moderation workers' status at MegaTech as limited-term, contract employees played directly into this situation. Josh said, "The contracted team, my team that is there for just a year, versus the team that is there full-time, like they constantly tell us 'you guys have just as much say in how our policy is shaped as we do.' And that's of course, not true at all . . . I mean, we do communicate about the policy, but we don't really have any kind of power over changing it."

Such lack of agency in determining policy for MegaTech's platform was not only a source of frustration for workers like Josh, whose tasks were relegated almost entirely to application of internal content policy, but it was a missed opportunity for MegaTech, which may have been able to determine a great deal about regional political strife or conflict, new and emerging trends in disturbing behaviors, and particularly pernicious and crafty manipulation of the platform by nefarious users, among other things—if only the feedback of their own commercial content moderation administrators had been sought or valued. By and large, it was not.

Global Diplomacy, MegaTech Style: Commercial Content Moderation's Invisible Foreign Policy Function

Often, videos that otherwise might have seemed to be in clear violation of policies became catalysts for arduous decision-making processes or heated debates among the moderation team members and between the moderators and SecPol. Many times, decisions were made not strictly based on the content of the videos. Instead, their value or merit as political commentary or advocacy was considered. The videos uploaded to MegaTech from war-torn parts of the globe were some of the most difficult that the team had to deal with, and all three of the participants cited this content as material that stayed with them after the workday was over.

The decisions made to keep this type of content up on the platform or to remove it had a major impact in the larger world because MegaTech is a major global distribution platform for people attempting to draw attention to all sorts of causes, including political crises, conflicts, and war crimes. Therefore, the decisions related to this type of material were treated seriously and somberly by both the MegaTech moderators and members of the SecPol team. In this way, MegaTech's policy decisions regarding which war-zone footage was suitable for hosting and dissemination and which was not—and, in fact, even in determining whether a conflict met the definition of a legitimate "war"—were powerful in ways often beyond what members of either team realized at first blush. This became particularly evident as MegaTech's platform began to serve more and more often as one of the few places that people involved in such conflicts could use to advocate or disseminate documentation of the crises occurring in their parts of the world. Max Breen recalled:

When I was there the Arab Spring stuff was happening, and a lot of that content was really gory. But then, that was the only place activists in those countries could upload it, so we let it go with a warning. Like, you had to say "I'm over 18" to see this video. For instance, if you have the monk who self-immolated in Vietnam, if it was documentary footage of that, even though it was disturbing, that would probably be fine. If it was inflammatory or taken out of context, then obviously someone committing suicide is not going to be acceptable or . . . like, Columbine is something that shows up on MegaTech a lot. If it is documentary footage it is fine, but there is a lot of mass shooter glorification stuff that happens there, and that's obviously not okay.

Even though such content might appear to violate Mega-Tech's prohibition against excessive gore, violence, or the harming of children, exceptions were often made based on guidelines issued by SecPol, full-time MegaTech employees all, and, possibly, from even higher than that; the content moderation administrators at MegaTech were not always privy to all aspects of the company's decision-making process. Internal policy governing the terms of access to user-generated content related to conflict and geopolitical strife reflected and was affected by the fickle and dynamic currents of world events and political allegiances. This dimension of policy, too, was easily identifiable as being developed through the lens of a U.S.-centric political perspective. It could very easily become a situation, therefore, of either tacitly or overtly supporting U.S. foreign policy by choosing which content would be displayed and which would be pulled down. Josh Santos explained:

There are things that regardless of the level of like how much you can stomach, there are things we see in a day that can completely catch you off guard. Especially things like the war in Syria right now, I mean, you never know what's going to come up. There was a day when there was a bomb in a school and it killed like twenty-some kids, and the video was devastating. There were just pieces of children everywhere. It was very raw. And because it was, we were trying to help by keeping things about their plight up, like we kept all that up. Just seeing that. And these videos become viral for that reason. Because they are very violent, and they are very relevant and topical. We've constantly seen this footage. That takes it out of you a little bit.

Josh questioned the policy that permitted content from some conflicts being allowed to stand, for informational and advocacy purposes, while other material was removed. Here, too, the power differential between the contractor admins, employed for a finite period and limited in their ability to craft or enact policy, and that of the SecPol team, full-timers who developed policy but were removed from the day-to-day realities of screening the content, came to a head once again. According to Josh:

One of the people on SecPol is very passionate about any kind of crisis in the Middle East, which is a fine position. But the thing is because we have such a sensitive approach to how we tackle videos in the Middle East, it doesn't translate to other nations. Which me and another admin got really

upset about that. For example, the drug war that is
going on in Mexico—a lot of the people who are
on both sides were uploading videos of the war.
Murders or hostages and interrogations. Stuff that
we keep up for the war that is going on in Syria.
The exact same content. I mean, it's for a different
reason, but the content is the same. There are two
sides, for all purposes it's the same content. But the
argument they gave me was that it wasn't newsworthy enough. The drug war! There was also a recent,
a coup or something in Russia, a civil war or something in a really small, isolated area. And the
violence out of there, they also said it wasn't newsworthy. It just feels like there is a double standard,
and my understanding is the sole purpose is that
one person on the SecPol team is just passionate
about the issues in the Middle East.

Caitlyn also struggled with the content from Syria, although she disavowed any longer-term effects from viewing the
video: "Most of the stuff that I've seen is just redundant and
I'm just like 'Okay. I know what that is. I'm over it.' But there's
always some really weird stuff that comes out that you've
never seen. Or just a lot of the, all the really graphic images
from Syria, those are still pretty bad. But they're fleeting. It's
only like a few seconds."

Effectively, the moderation admins were serving a powerful editorial role at MegaTech, although their relative invisibility, lack of power with regard to influencing internal content
policies, and the inability of end users to meaningfully engage
with, or even perceive, either policies or procedures under which
MegaTech governed user-generated content meant that the

editorial role bore little resemblance to analogs in other media contexts. Further, it was not always clear that the commercial content moderation administrators at MegaTech were in a position to make such decisions effectively or with appropriate context.

Such was the situation in which Caitlyn found herself. Although she was tasked with making decisions about keeping war-zone content up and accessible to millions of people or removing it, Caitlyn appeared to have little knowledge about the nature of the conflicts she was seeing and reviewing, the parties involved, or the implications of the footage uploaded to MegaTech. When I asked if this job had brought her more awareness of global conflicts and events she had been previously unfamiliar with, she replied, "Yeah, it's more like, though, I'd have to really like read up on the stuff outside [of work] because we see all the original content, but I still don't really understand what's happening and I'd have to, like, make an effort. And all that just seems so complicated that even if I tried, I'd still be pretty confused."

Despite her lack of confidence about her knowledge and ability to understand the context and meaning of conflict-zone footage, Caitlyn was still charged with its review and adjudication, with little more than internal MegaTech policies and any additional edicts from SecPol to guide her. Like Josh, she too saw a disconnect between the internal policies involving some of the content decisions concerning this type of material. Yet in our interview she confessed to not having enough information to understand or evaluate the rationale behind them. Instead, she complied with the MegaTech policies as dictated to her.

> Well, most of [the war-zone footage], we have to keep most of it up, actually like all of it. Because

we're seen as, like, their way to show what's happening there. Even though if it was happening in other countries, like in Mexico with all the drug war stuff? That stuff we would have to take down, 'cause I guess, like, I don't know the reasoning for that. But in Syria it's just like we're giving them this voice. We age-restrict a lot of the really graphic stuff. But some of the stuff where's there's just a dead body but they're not bleeding or something—anyone can see it. But also the people who search for it are from the area and it's in Arabic so I don't know how many people, if they're a lot of Arabic people in the U.S. or kids that are searching for it, so they're not going to come across it. Which makes me feel better about keeping it up.

Meanwhile, the brand management and protection function was often at the center of the decision to allow or remove other kinds of political content, too—often on the orders of SecPol or other upper-management teams. Brand management in these cases served not only to insulate MegaTech itself from criticism, but also to protect its partners and high-volume users from negative publicity. In our interview, Josh referred to this aspect of commercial content moderation as a "PR," or "public relations," concern.

The policy is so slow to change, [the SecPol team members] don't really have much work to do, so they are constantly like, they just have a bunch of semantic arguments every day. And they just kind of, they're not really changing much. They are clearly working on something, but nothing much changes because of them. Only when there is a clear policy issue or a legal issue, for example before [we had] our foreign terror organization policy we would just allow Al-Qaeda to have their videos up. And then as soon as an article comes out, I think in the *New York Times,* "Oh, MegaTech is working with Al-Qaeda" or "MegaTech is allowing Al-Qaeda to upload their videos." That instantly becomes a PR issue, and then our policy team says, "Okay, we have to make a policy about this." But basically, unless there is a pertinent PR or legal issue our policy does not change. That team is there to protect MegaTech, so we'll allow anything to be up unless it is becoming a PR or a legal issue.

At MegaTech, issues of public relations and brand management were conflated with, were influenced by, and, in turn, themselves influenced issues of democratic expression and political advocacy. Yet most users attempting to harness the power of the MegaTech platform for advocacy had no real grasp of the ramifications of the decision-making process behind the hosting of their content, or that it was often evaluated primarily through the lens of MegaTech's brand protection worries. Because of its massive popularity, ubiquity, and ease of use, MegaTech continues to be a site where people from around the world upload graphic material with the goal of achieving support or to advocate for a political faction or group in war or conflict. Without any other real alternative space for such material that can be used with the ubiquity and ease of the Mega-Tech platform and at the same scale, and with governments and others that have extraordinary interests in curbing access to the internet as a vital part of controlling conflicts, people, and societies, MegaTech will undoubtedly continue to have an out-sized role in effecting influence in these arenas, primarily based on what it does or does not allow to be shared on its platform.

It is a complicated and fraught relationship, and although MegaTech's internal policies may seem to favor people in crisis seeking outlets to ask for the world's support and to incite outrage over their plights, it must be underscored that Mega-Tech's allegiances ultimately lie elsewhere. Even when individuals in the company attempt to bolster the content of people seeking support and advocacy, as with the SecPol employee, Josh and Caitlyn both perceived an unequal application of policies to material that, content-wise, was very similar. When a commercial, profit-driven platform like MegaTech stands in for democratic access to information dissemination, such confusions over allegiances and goals will necessarily feud with drives to maintain positive corporate relations with shareholders and governments. Yet, in a time of digital enclosure and vast commercialization of zones of expression, where such zones exist at all, it is not clear what other options people might have to voice dissent.

Online Crime-Stoppers: The MegaTech Underbelly and Commercial Content Moderation's Engagement with Law Enforcement

Although I never directly asked any of the commercial content moderation team members about the very worst of the content they had come across in their tenure at MegaTech, such topics invariably surfaced in the course of our conversations. In each case, the workers identified their difficulty with seeing graphic depictions of sexual abuse involving children, cases of self-harm threats, and footage from war zones as the most traumatic that they dealt with. When they witnessed what they believed to be crimes, the contractors on MegaTech's content moderation team had specific protocols for engaging with law enforcement and other partners to provide information on the content creators and uploaders, and, when possible, those in harm's way. Max discussed the way this protocol functioned and his experiences dealing with it as he advanced in his position to tackling more challenging commercial content moderation cases:

> There were specific queues for various languages, for instance, that you would escalate out of Tier 1. So like if there was one [video] all in Hungarian and you couldn't tell what was going on, you could send it to the Hungarian queue. There was a dedicated spam queue. There was Tier 2, which was any time one of the admins were not sure what the call was or something that maybe should be left up but violated some policy—one that we would use to discuss whether that policy was broken or not. There was the child porn queue, which anything from Tier 1 that needed to be reported to the National Center for Missing and Exploited Children would get funneled into. And a couple others. Once you started doing those, your quantity of videos started going down, but I would reliably do about 1,500 to 2,000 a day. . . .
>
> NCMEC is the National Center for Missing and Exploited Children. We had a direct connection with them . . . we were able to just hit a hot key and it would forward the video and all the data and information associated with that video straight to NCMEC. Oh, and if anything was a suicide threat

or something that required immediate attention or
in some cases was what would become news a couple hours later, we would send that to the team
above ours, [SecPol]. They wrote all the policy, although they took input from us, they reached out
to law enforcement or the big-name partners or
things like that.

There was a resulting sense of altruism and self-sacrifice,
of doing something for a greater good, that kept Max and the
other content moderators going at MegaTech when they encountered the worst material.[2] These difficult moments were
made slightly less so by a feeling among the workers that their
interventions could make a difference; their reports to law
enforcement might lead to an arrest or to a child being removed
from danger. I asked Max if, when he was doing content moderation work, he felt like he had a duty or sense of responsibility in what he was doing in terms of mitigating damage to
others.

Absolutely that was one of the things that helped
you not just quit immediately. Especially for the
child porn and child abuse material. Because most
of the time it would be re-uploads, unfortunately—
stuff that was already known to NCMEC and the
FBI. But every once and awhile you'd get someone
that was dumb enough to upload new firsthand
content. And it was horrible to have to see, and
those were always the worst days, but at the same
time you knew that you had a direct line to law
enforcement that could handle that. And one of
the things that helped the most actually, with

dealing with that kind of content, is we had a video conference with a guy from INTERPOL who handled that kind of stuff in Europe. . . . And they were showing how they found within a day a kid that was uploaded to Photobucket [an online social media image-sharing site] or something. And it's this totally average looking ten-year-old kid sitting in a totally average ten-year-old kid's bedroom. There's nothing, no written text that would indicate country, no data that would tell when it was taken, anything, and the researchers found, poking out from under the bed, a bag with a company logo on it that only was a regional grocery store in northeastern France. And from that they were able to find this kid and get him out of there in like a day or two.

Despite the personal and professional gratification that came from intervening to save a child making the work bearable for Max and his teammates, there was not a consistent mechanism or feedback loop for them to get updates about positive outcomes. Max wished that this were the case, although it is likely that both the protected status of the harmed child, as well as law enforcement investigations, precluded such information from being shared. Max recalled, "We never got any feedback, and that's another thing I said in my exit interview, anytime someone sends a report in, be it a suicide threat or child abuse or something that there is a tangible benefit from, oh my God, tell them. It will make their lives so much better. But even knowing that that kind of thing was feasible from this content that was virtually anonymous, just knowing that that could happen really helped you deal with it."

During his tenure with the commercial content moderation team, Josh also encountered situations that mandated the involvement of law enforcement. In his case, these experiences were based on video content expressing suicidal threats and ideation. His ability to streamline the MegaTech content moderation workflow to evoke a potentially lifesaving intervention was one of his points of pride. According to Josh, "Our team has been very proactive when it comes to people leaving suicidal messages. Basically, the process to escalate any suicidal message to the authorities is really cumbersome, so I basically inserted a much quicker system. A lot more admins actually took the time to escalate any of the suicidal videos. So that helped, I mean, it's a very low number, but any prevention helps. Like I think we prevented nine suicides. According to the authorities. Out of like eight hundred suicidal videos. But whatever, nine people."

At that point, Josh paused before expressing some of the most profound insights he displayed in our lengthy interview. Josh implicated the very existence of MegaTech as a potential cause to lead someone to depression and suicidal thoughts, due to its nature as a magnet for disturbing content, bullying activity, and people with disturbed mental states. Josh, in effect, implicated himself, his colleagues, MegaTech's corporate environment, and, most important, all of us who use MegaTech and platforms similar to it.

> I mean, we get feedback only when the outcome is positive. That's the other thing I'm wondering about. We'll get feedback when the authorities say, "Oh, congratulations, we helped this person that uploaded this [suicide threat] video and they are getting treatment now." But I have always been

curious . . . what about the people you don't report back on? Are they okay? What about people who haven't been flagged yet, people who put a suicide video up and no one flagged, 'cause we're not seeing those? And then, to me it's a little frustrating that every time, it's good that our team is proactive when it comes to people leaving up suicidal messages, but at the same time, we are MegaTech. Which is probably a catalyst for making a lot of people want to commit suicide. So that's something they are not bringing up. Yeah, this person feels like they are bullied, but they also feel like they are bullied because of our website. Like because we're not really tackling these [abusive] commenters [on MegaTech]. I don't know. But that's something that people keep hush-hush. They don't really want to think about that side of it.

He continued, his cynicism and frustration clear in his delivery:

I would say personally one of my pet peeves is when people are on a high horse and people are kind of congratulating themselves all the time because I'm like, yeah, it's good to be proud of yourself but at the same time, step back a little bit. But at MegaTech that sentiment is so widespread. Everyone is so proud of themselves at MegaTech. Everyone is just smelling their own farts. When someone is like "We prevented a suicide!" and everyone is just "Good job guys!" I agree, good job guys, but it's like let's take a step back and think about why this happened in the first place.

This was one of the only moments in which a commercial content moderation worker from MegaTech directly connected its business model—the reliance on a constant stream of user-generated content to draw eyeballs and attention from its user base—to the negative outcomes of the seemingly inevitable appearance of violent and abusive content on its platform. In other words, Josh recognized MegaTech's role not only in cleaning up abusive content, but in having solicited it in the first place.

"You Dwell on It": On Job Stress, Isolation, and Impacts

The commercial content moderators I have spoken with over the years have often described a strategy of self-segregation from friends and family and didn't want to talk to others outside their work teams about the job, in part because doing so, in their minds, would have burdened others. The long-term impacts of the work are totally unknown; if longitudinal psychological studies have been done on populations of commercial content moderators, they have not been made public. Yet it stands to reason that being exposed to such material day in and day out might have deleterious effects on one's psyche. The workers at MegaTech dealt with these pressures by supporting one another as well as they could. During Max's tenure, supportive talk among his team was a key coping strategy. Max said, "Everyone [on the admin team] was very talkative and being talkative helped you—not necessarily to deal with the content, we didn't really talk too much about the problematic stuff—but it helped distract you. Without being able to talk to other people all day long and be able to distract yourself from this, [you] couldn't do it. It's awful. But I got along very well with all the people on my team and I'm still friendly with a great deal of them, and it was a good support structure even if we didn't actually talk about the videos themselves for the most part."

Despite Max's claims that the job took very little emotional or physical toll on him, he contradicted this assertion by noting his weight gain and increased alcoholic beverage consumption during his time at MegaTech, as well as struggling outside of work with thoughts of specific images or videos he had seen on the job.

> I handle stress okay. I thought I handled it better than I did once I got the job. But once I was a couple months into the job, even though the content was mostly the same, it's the accumulation. It weighs on you. But I handle stress pretty well, I never let it impact me at work. I gained a lot of weight because I was snacking a bunch and probably drinking a lot more than I am now, but it never got to me too bad. Except in the time around the Arab Spring stuff, 'cause there was just so much gore coming out of there. That hit me pretty hard. But for the most part, the team was what really helped me deal with it the most. I wouldn't have been able to do it with a less talkative, friendly team.

These contradictory and revelatory moments in the interview were important, and they happened over and over again with all three MegaTech contractors. The workers assured and reassured me verbally that they were not negatively affected by their work, and then moments later would demonstrate, via anecdotes or other examples of difficult moments, that the work, in fact, was entering into their psyche and interpersonal relationships outside the bounds of their shifts.

This lack of self-awareness was curious; what was to be gained by insisting that one was unaffected by content that would likely cause most people difficulty? Of course, a main criterion of success for being good at this job was the ability to handle and manage the content. Admitting otherwise was, effectively, admitting to not having the skills to manage and master the job. Josh and Caitlyn, too, talked around the psychological and other impacts on themselves throughout our interviews. At various points, Josh described his attitude as one of "apathy" toward the disturbing content to which he was regularly exposed. And yet, just as in Max's case, it was clear that his moderation tasks did weigh upon him, at least from time to time, as they did on Caitlyn. Josh stated:

> For me, something that will really get to me, during a violent video is, like, noises. If I have to hear someone screaming or if I have to hear someone crying during something violent, that gets me more than the on-camera blood or gore. The fact that I don't have to listen to it, I can just look at pictures of it [as thumbnails], that makes it a lot easier—the moderator's iron constitution. I don't know, my job isn't difficult. It's just how much you can take in, how much you can handle. How much violence. And I mean even the violence isn't difficult. The violence and the porn don't get to me. It's just the things that people do, like the hate speech and the conspiracies.

For Josh and Caitlyn, in particular, who had been at her job for just three months, the reluctance to overtly address the results of the content viewing could have been a coping mechanism. Max, at a year removed from his experiences, had had more time to reflect, as well as to weigh the impacts of his content moderation job on other aspects of his life, in a way that Josh and Caitlyn perhaps had not been able to allow themselves to do yet. This aspect of the long-term implications of commercial content moderation on its workers must therefore be followed and studied after the workers have left their positions and moved on in their lives. As Caitlyn said, "A lot of the stuff hasn't been an issue for me, like a lot of the graphic like violent content hasn't been as serious as for other people. Cause for me it's like fleeting. I don't watch the videos. I can tell what's happening and I see it for a second. But then there have been some moments when I saw something really disturbing and I just have to take a break and like talk to someone on the team and be like 'this is really gross, I need to go back to normal life and just . . . you know, refresh.' "

During Max's time at MegaTech, the camaraderie and solidarity among the contractors on his team were key to his ability to complete his work tasks. Yet, by the time of Josh's tenure, the environment in the group had changed significantly and for the worse. Josh attributed this to a great deal of turnover, as mandated by the year-long contracts, and low morale, brought on, in part, by the knowledge that the emotionally tough commercial content moderation job was likely to end in termination, rather than in an elevation of status or promotion internally as a MegaTech full-timer, and the internal competition this engendered on the team. The change was significant, because the cohesive team environment had been a primary support structure for handling the difficult parts of the job. Without it, MegaTech's commercial content moderation team members lacked a crucial coping mechanism for the worst aspects of their tasks. Max said, "I can't imagine anyone who does [this] job and is able to just walk out at the end of their shift and just be done. You dwell on it, whether you want to or not. So that was something we were all conscious of and like I said, we never talked about it directly, but it definitely was a feature in the conversation subconsciously. So we'd chat after work or we'd go get a pub quiz, stay after work and play board games sometimes. It was just we all got along really well, and there was a sense of bonding because we were all dealing with the same thing."

Just a year later, the climate had declined dramatically, predicated in no small part by the sense of insecurity that their status as contractors provoked. Josh reported:

> When I started, there was a lot more camaraderie. There was more of a sentiment that we are all in this together. That kind of dissipated after certain people left, and it never really recovered. Right now, it's more cliquey I would say. Certain people kind of get along with others, but the team, as a whole, doesn't resonate. You can kind of tell during lunch hour. Before we would all go get lunch and no one would really speak to each other. And now we don't even get lunch together. Like two people will go get lunch and then two other people will go. So our team has . . . it's a very sad place because you really are trying to . . . and it's just because people are taking things personally . . . But really I think that the prime reason that we are the way we are is just because of the competitiveness. If there was a very clear understanding from the get-go that you will most likely not be working here after your

contract or if there was more opportunity for employment after your contract it would be a different story. But I feel that because everyone wants to get that, we call it red badges and white badges—so the red badges are the contractors and the white badge is the sought-after badge . . . everyone wants that white badge. I don't know. I feel like, as you can tell, I gave up on the concept of getting a job at MegaTech. At least immediately following the contract. But a lot of people hang on to it and disregard their co-workers for the sake of their own professional advancement. So long story short, the team environment could be better. It could be more.

"In the Hole of Filth": Effects of the Job on the Workers and the People in Their Lives

As with almost all the commercial content moderation workers I spoke with, from a variety of sectors, the MegaTech moderation team was particularly concerned with the potential for burdening others (such as friends and family members) if they were to tell them of their workplace experiences. Instead of sharing their experiences and their emotional responses to difficult content, the workers turned inward, either focusing such discussions only among one another, or not discussing them in a serious way at all.

Max found he had difficulty bringing his intimate partner, with whom he lived, into his work world, and preferred to isolate her from it. When I asked him if he spoke about any of his experiences in dealing with the videos with anyone else in his life outside of work, he responded:

Mostly in a joking manner. I would tell them about the funny things I saw or maybe the serious things I saw but that were newsworthy or relevant. I'd try not to talk about stuff that no one ever wants to see, ever. And no one should have to even hear about. I tried not to discuss that with anyone. And I should have. Because that's really something . . . I wouldn't ever want to lay more stuff on my co-workers that were also dealing with that, but I should have had someone I could talk to about it. Like my girlfriend told me, who I live with and lived with at the time, you know, I would come home after a bad day and have a bunch of beer or something and she would say, "Oh, you should talk about it." And I knew that I should but at the same time I didn't want to burden someone else with it. Which is I think how everyone on the team felt.

Josh felt the disconnect from other people most acutely when he would encounter friends, or meet new people in his life, when the talk would turn to everyone's work. Not only was it unpleasant to discuss with others, he found the talk was often reductive or superficial in a way that did not reflect his work reality. It was a reality he preferred to allow the uninitiated to avoid. As he put it,

People are very interested in what you do when you tell someone you work at MegaTech. They are like "what do you do at MegaTech?" "Oh, I moderate all the heinous content, the porn." And people find that funny or interesting, so you just give them a cute little summary. Like, "Yeah, I see porn all day," or "yeah, I see bloody gore all day." And they are like, "Oh, that's disappointing." But I don't really go into the nitty-gritty ... they're really just interested in the content, what you're watching. So that's pretty much what I limit it to. Or I tell them just about the perks of the job. You don't really want to talk about it. You kind of feel like you spent eight hours just in this hole of filth that you don't really want to bring it into the rest of your life. Even when I'm with my co-workers we don't talk about anything work related. We just kind of keep it ... it's not so much that it's traumatizing. It's just that, I don't know, you don't want to pass your burden on other people's shoulders.

Caitlyn, too, kept her concerns and viewing-related difficulties within the commercial content moderation team, for similar reasons, in spite of her claims that she was largely unaffected by her work: "I've really liked the people I've met. They make it a lot better and easier to do. 'Cause you just can't talk to your friends about this because they're not there. They'd be like, 'What? That's weird.' When you're with people that know what you're going through, it makes it a lot better."

Partners, friends, and even acquaintances were largely off the table as informal support mechanisms to the MegaTech mods. Despite the lack of comprehensive health insurance for its moderation contractors, MegaTech had made some tacit attempts to address the potential of psychological stress and difficulty handling content on the workers. Yet that attempt had mostly failed. Max stated:

I know now they have counselors come in. I'm not sure at what intervals or how effective it is. When I was hired they said we were supposed to have some kind of access to counseling as part of the contract. Because we didn't have insurance, that was not part of the contract, but it was supposed to be provided, but I was never told how to access it, and as far as I know no one ever did. My last month there they started doing, they had a counselor come in once, but it was two weeks before I left so I don't know what ever came of it. It was a group session, I don't know if they did or do individual sessions. But I would, in my exit interview I told my manager, and I would advocate this to any company that has to deal with this kind of content, you need, you don't need to offer that to the people, you need to force them to do it. Because I would imagine other people in other companies doing this have the mindset that me and my teammates did—that, even a professional, you don't want to burden them with all the horrible stuff you have to look at all day long. Because they may be helping you deal with it, but then they have to deal with that too. And even secondhand it's damaging.

Facing lack of mental health care at work and a lack of support in his private life, Max described how the stress of the job took a serious toll on his relationship with his partner.

At one point, after the Arab Spring stuff and after I'd been there nine or ten months, I was already looking for other work at this point, I was pretty fed up, it's like one of the only breakdown/ meltdown things I can remember in my life. I tried to break up with my girlfriend. She wouldn't let me, basically. She said, "You have to give me a reason," and we sat there and talked and [I] realized I was just redirecting problems with my job at her. Because I wasn't talking about them to anyone. It was a mess. And I should have been talking to someone about them earlier, but you don't want to lay it on someone else.

A year later, not much had changed. Max's suggestions to mandate psychological counseling had not been implemented; it was still on a limited schedule and considered voluntary. Josh reported:

We get a bi-monthly visit from a psychologist. And they talk to us in a group or we have the option to talk one-on-one. But most people have other means of escape. There is not a script for work protocol, so you can leave your desk whenever you want and just come back whenever you want, so someone will just get up and go somewhere, take a smoke break. I would say dealing with the content, we don't really rely on each other to get over it. We might say something in passing, like "I saw this really gross video about this," but then we're just venting.

Caitlyn's limited experience with the corporate counseling staff seemed to make it even more difficult for her to cope with the stress of her job, as she preferred to leave the elements of the work she found difficult undiscussed and felt uncomfortable dealing with the in-house psychological services on the occasions that they were made available to her. In part, this was because of the relationship the mental health professionals had to MegaTech itself. Caitlyn was distrustful about discussing any trouble she may have been having coping with her job while on the job, an unsurprising reaction when coping skills are key to succeeding as a professional content screener.

> There's these people that come in every few months or something, but they kind of, when we had that meeting talking about stress, I was more stressed after, it like ruined my mood. I was like, "Why did I go to this?" I think some people have been upset that they don't have more services, but I don't think I really need them because I'm pretty fine. I wasn't really comfortable with the speakers. I guess they're just, it was really forced to talk about these things. And it became like, everyone was just complaining about the job. And I didn't trust the two psychologists. I was just like, "Who are you hippy-dippy people just coming in, trying to make us talk about all our feelings and stuff we didn't like ever verbalize, and, I don't like you guys." I just wanted to be like, I don't know. I was in a great mood before, and then in the beginning I just had this, what is that, fight-or-flight instinct to leave. But I didn't cause I wanted to be polite. I should have said, "Eff social convention," 'cause I knew the meeting, I could tell it was just going to stress me out. But I didn't leave.

Because of the moderators' status as contract workers, they did not receive regular employee health benefits from MegaTech, or from their third-party contracting firms either.

In the United States, until recently and prior to the Affordable Care Act, passed in 2010 and put into effect in 2014, access to health care and insurance has almost exclusively been related to employment status. For lower-wage workers and workers in other than full-time, permanent positions, even when such insurance benefits were offered, the policies were often priced out of reach for those workers, and many therefore went without insurance. With recent changes in U.S. policy regarding health care still coming into effect and constantly under threat, it remains to be seen what kinds of results it will hold for workers like the MegaTech moderation contractors. Even so, the kind of care they most need, as a result of their jobs, is mental health care, which may continue to be out of financial reach for many, even those who hold health insurance. Further, even when such care is available and affordable, the stigma associated with seeking it out (as described by the workers themselves) means that many do not seek out mental health support or treatment for fear of what the acknowledgment of the need for care might mean about themselves or to others. During the interviews, I was sensitive to the material the workers had likely seen and conveyed my sensitivity to it when it was appropriate. In response, Max said,

> Horror movies are ineffective at this point. I've seen all that stuff in real life. . . . It's permanently damaging. I will never forget a lot of that stuff. And I don't dwell on it this point down the road, it's not something that two years on is, oh God, it's only been a year, hasn't it? I don't dwell on it daily, I don't dwell on it weekly, I wouldn't even say monthly, but every once in awhile, I couldn't even sit down and remember what some horrible videos

I saw were, but every once and a while you remember: "Oh, I saw a video about this" or similar to this. This one time my girlfriend and I were fooling around on the couch or something and she made a joke involving a horse. And I'd seen horse porn earlier in the day and I just shut down. Okay. Goodnight, I'm done. It's just these weird things that come out of nowhere. Rarely at this point. But I doubt, maybe a decade down the line, maybe I will stop encountering these things that bring it up, but who knows?

The Revolving Door: MegaTech's Corporate Culture and the Commercial Content Moderation Contractor Structure

A company like MegaTech has vast wealth and resources available to it to hire virtually whomever it feels it has a business need for. Therefore, the decision for companies to structure a commercial content moderation team as only limited-term, third-party contractors must be understood as calculated and deliberate, and done to achieve desired ends. I talked to the workers about what they suspected might be the reasons for that decision.

Do I want to think [the companies are] benevolent or not? If they're benevolent: because no one should do this job for more than a year. No one. Realistically speaking, we're a very important part of that company that is underappreciated, and if you had full-time employees, and you know they

pay us a lot but that is coming from someone who
was just out of college and didn't have any experience with that . . . if you had those same people getting paid that same wage for years they wouldn't do
it. They'd strike or they'd quit. The point is you
would run into problems after two years, maybe
three. It's not a healthy work environment and you
need to have rotation or the department is going to
collapse in on itself. Whether it's organizing to get a
better deal or breakdown. . . . There was actually a
really awesome article about [commercial content
moderation workers] when I was working at Mega-
Tech, I think they were interviewing the moderators for MySpace. And they were the ones in the
shitty cubicles in Florida [working] for eight bucks
an hour. And I remember that getting passed
around the internet with people wondering how
many people there are like that—and there are so
many of us and we're all unhappy.

Josh's rationale for MegaTech's contractor-hiring motives
was similar to that of Max's. He explained his perspective in
detail:

MegaTech's reasoning for it is that psychologically
it is not something you should do for longer than a
year. And that's evident with the people who have a
second contract. They have to wait three months
before they decide to work again. I mean, I can't
imagine . . . if this was, if I had the option of doing
this full time I probably would. And that is not because it is enjoyable. But for me it is a stress-free

job. I mean, this has been one of the least stressful years of my life. Just because I have been so comfortable with the job. So I would keep working there even though I've demonstrated a pretty fair level of apathy towards what I do.

Assuredly, burnout due to the constant viewing of troubling content was a factor among the commercial content moderation workers at MegaTech and elsewhere, as was burnout due to the rote, routine, and factory-like nature of the work.

Yet there are a number of other reasons that MegaTech may have found for the arrangement of using precarious, temporary employees of third-party firms for their mission-critical commercial content moderation functions. Both Max and Josh cited the potential for psychological harm to the workers (while still being reluctant to articulate the harm that may have been done to them in their work environment). Max, too, acknowledged that one-year finite tours as contractors, generating constant turnover and little uniformity in management or loyalty to a particular firm, served as a foil to the kind of environment that would prove fertile ground for moderation worker organizing for better conditions or pay at MegaTech.

By precluding terms longer than one year, offering a total possible two years of work in commercial content moderation, mandating a three-month break in between contracts, and using, at times, up to three different contract companies to supply workers, MegaTech ensured a fractured team of content screeners with little long-term investment in the firm. Likewise, MegaTech returned the favor to the moderators via lesser status and lower pay. Finally, it was easy for MegaTech to describe these workers as temporary and having never been a part of the MegaTech employment team, a fact that might come in handy down the road if any of the moderation contractors who worked at MegaTech were to allege harm from their tenure. Josh had his suspicions about MegaTech knowing that its moderation employees could be subject to burnout due to the relentless demands of the job.

> I think the real reason is that you kind of get burned out. And after a year, certain things slow you down workwise. When I started, like my first few months, after I learned the policy really well, that's really when I peaked. I would say like four or five months in. It was when I had very clear knowledge of our policies and what I was expected to do, but as you keep working there and there is more discussion on certain policies or there is new edge cases that are brought up, like the more you kind of evaluate the policies and the more new things come that kind of topple what you've learned, you start to be more cautious and you go more slower. I'd say after a year you are not performing at your best. That might be another reason why. You definitely become more comfortable, you start slowing down. Especially with the contract jobs.

While MegaTech was, and continues to be, one of the most successful internet companies of all time and is notorious for its lush working conditions and endless perks, the commercial content moderation contractors inhabited another status at MegaTech that denied them many of these benefits. Most critical in the case of the team was the lack of health care, the mechanism by which they could have sought outside psychological counseling had they so desired, if not fully paid for, then perhaps with some assistance. Instead, MegaTech provided periodic visits from a mental health counselor brought in by the company and offered voluntarily to the admin team. Few people made use of this service. Yet by supplying the counselor, MegaTech was able to claim a bare minimum of due diligence in attempting to deal with employee mental health needs, while simultaneously distancing itself from the results of the job on the employees, as they were not and likely never would be MegaTech full-timers. In this way, MegaTech enacted a series of distancing moves designed to create a plausible deniability to limit their responsibility for any workplace harm, particularly when such harm may take time to show up—months or even years after the termination of the contract.

It is commonplace in the information technology world that contractors and subcontractors working for huge tech firms frequently inhabit the lower echelons of work, both in status and pay (in such areas as quality assurance, information technology support and help desk functions, and so on). Indeed, these workers provide the originator of the contract with an ability to quickly ramp up or ramp down a workforce without having to bring them fully into their operation. But just as in the cases where these firms contract and subcontract aspects of the manufacturing process to other parts of the world and are then able to claim little control over them or little responsibility for them, workers, such as those of MegaTech's commercial content moderation team, exist in a similarly liminal territory, with the added confusion of being housed side-by-side with their higher-status counterparts.

True, too, was the fact that the contract status itself served as a source of dissatisfaction and frustration for the contractors on the MegaTech moderation team. Josh described his feelings at the close of the year, taking on the myth of the Silicon Valley tech corporation as a fun or enjoyable place to be.

MegaTech's supposed to be one of those places that doesn't feel like it has a strong corporate vibe, but it still exists. At the end of the day there's still a bottom line, and a feeling of being a cog rather than a catalyst for change in the company, especially from the position of the contractor. And little things like contractors, just because they are contractors, get far fewer amenities. The full-time employees give you a different attitude just because you are a contractor. It doesn't give me any feeling of security for the corporate structure in general. I feel like regardless of how modern or how quirky you want to present your corporation, there's still that sense that you have one role to fulfill and very little vertical mobility. You don't feel like part of a team, you feel part of a structure—one little piece that isn't recognized. MegaTech didn't really do much to make me feel otherwise. . . . I mean the propaganda's there. You always hear that Wal-Mart brainwashes their employees to think such-and-such ways, but that exists at MegaTech too.

"Low-Hanging Fruit": MegaTech and Global Commercial Content Moderation Outsourcing

When Max Breen began his employment at MegaTech, outsourcing commercial content moderation work to other parts of the world and other worksite configurations seemed like an unthinkable proposition. Max explained his opposition to that practice to me.

> You know, man, outsourcing in general is such a mess. In terms of our specific content, I don't think it works because anywhere that is going to hire or provide employees for the price these companies want to pay, they're going to be in places like India or the Philippines.... The culture is so dramatically different when you are trying to apply a policy that is based on a United States or Western Europe culture: it doesn't work. They tried outsourcing to India before I was there, and it was such a disaster that they just canceled it and said we have to do this all in-house.... [The Indian contractors] would be removing pictures of people at the beach with their family in bikinis, because they are like, that's not appropriate for public consumption. In very narrow terms of content moderation for a Western site, the outsourcing—they are going to be drastically underpaying, I can't imagine doing the job for less than they paid me. They paid me a decent amount, and it was still miserable. I can't imagine doing it for nothing. That was one of the only perks. We didn't get benefits. It was really draining and brutal.

Despite Max's belief that outsourcing to India or other parts of the world would cause havoc for MegaTech, the firm had, a year on, pursued this very strategy. MegaTech still had its in-house contract moderation team but also employed call center/business process outsourcing in other parts of the world to augment the in-house group and break apart moderation tasks into lower- and higher-order ones. Josh Santos revealed another more frustrating problem with the outsourcing: the damage it was causing to the on-site contractors' metrics, or measures by which their job performance was evaluated. He describes this issue:

> About four months into my contract we out-sourced all of the so-called low-hanging-fruit vid-eos, which are spam and pornography. Things that instantly, it takes you a half second to recognize, you don't have to watch the video. 'Cause things like hate speech or someone sitting in front of a web cam talking for like, let's say, the duration of the video is fifteen minutes and it says something like "Jews control such-and-such." You have no idea what this guy's going to say. If it's going to be hate speech or if it's conspiracy talk, so you actually have to watch those, whereas if it is pornography or spam it is instantly recognizable. We took all of those videos, which are most of our videos, I would say 60 to 70 percent of our stuff is spam and porn, and that all went to our team in India. So after that happened we had less than half the volume that we used to have. And so that just, that ruined our met-rics. 'Cause that was something we were rated on: how much videos we do. And all of a sudden, we have to find a new variable to test an admin's com-petency. 'Cause now that we don't have these "low-hanging fruit" we have way less volume.

Josh shared Max's worry that outsourcing to elsewhere in the world would lead to declining quality in the commercial content moderation work being done. His description and Max's highlighted the tension inherent in the transglobal partnering with outsourcing groups in different parts of the world and coming from different cultural, social, and linguistic contexts. According to Josh,

> All [Management] did was separate the queues. They all used to go to just one queue, and then we separated the porn queue and the spam queue, so basically India takes care of those. We have the option to go into those queues but then India would have nothing to do, because we would destroy that queue in moments. I don't understand why but they didn't train the India team as thoroughly as they trained our team so, I don't know, they just have, they go through the queue a little slower. I don't understand why they didn't train them. . . . I don't know, I feel like they don't trust them quite yet to make the policy. And I mean there are a number of reasons for that. They are a brand-new team. Just cultural differences. Like you notice there are things the India team takes down that are fine. Or a lot of things they leave up that are not fine. And there are just cultural differences.

An Internet Without Commercial Content Moderation

I once asked Max Breen whether he could imagine a MegaTech without people doing the work he did. "No," he answered. "It would be 100 percent porn. [laughter] One hundred percent.

It would be a train wreck. The awful part is, it has to be done. It can't not be moderated. But there's no good way to do it."

Even in light of Josh's consistent cynicism and dark outlook on professional moderation work and his time at MegaTech throughout our interview, his closing words were strangely optimistic, in a sense; in them, he revealed a powerful ability to take the difficult content he internalized and turn it into a positive reflection on the human condition. Josh's outlook may have been part of the key to his capability to muster a year serving as a commercial content moderator on MegaTech's team.

> Despite the amount of violence I was exposed to this year . . . it was almost, I am just like in awe of humanity. . . . Because every time I thought that there's no way someone will trump the heinousness, someone would. Like you think it couldn't get any darker and then the next day you would see something darker. I mean, half the videos we see are fine. Like they're not violating a policy at all, so a lot of time I would see very creative stuff. It taught me to view humanity, to not take, to recognize there really are no limits to what the human mind can think of and accomplish. Because I have definitely seen things that in a million years I would never have expected a person to say or do. Good and bad. So it definitely gave me an almost uplifting . . . something to see how diverse we are.

Living in the San Francisco Bay area, which includes Silicon Valley, where many technology, social media, and internet companies have their headquarters, has become infamously expensive, prohibitive even, as it was throughout 2012, the time of my interviews with the MegaTech mods. In 2016, median one-bedroom apartment rents were as high as $3,920 per month.[3] By 2018, in nearby Palo Alto, the home of the world's first trillion-dollar company, Apple, the median home value was over $3 million.[4] Living costs in the Bay Area and Silicon Valley have become out of reach for even salaried employees, with six-figure incomes proving inadequate to provide housing for a family of four.[5] Meanwhile, the work of the three MegaTech commercial content mods featured in this chapter earned them just shy of $50,000 during their year-long contract for their mission-critical service to the MegaTech platform. And after that year, they would be out of a job in one of the most expensive places to live in the world, through MegaTech's revolving door of in-house contractors with little to show for it other than a line on their résumés and exposure to a side of humanity that they would try, in vain, to forget.

4

"I Call Myself a Sin-Eater"

There really is no free speech on commercial sites.
—Rick Reilly

OnlineExperts: A Boutique in the Cloud

At the time of our meeting, Rick Reilly was a fifty-five-year-old white Canadian expatriate living in Mexico. A former wireless executive, he had retired from one career and then moved into management of a commercial content management company at the behest of a friend and former co-worker, the founder of a startup, OnlineExperts. OnlineExperts was a boutique firm offering full-service content moderation and social media management. After first declining to join his friend's new venture, Rick eventually longed for the challenge of building a business in a new and growing sector.[1]

Rick is an affable and kind man who evinced a very client-oriented perspective. The beliefs he had developed in his years as an executive shone through in his outlook and thinking about commercial content moderation and OnlineExperts' practices and policies. Thoughtful and introspective, Rick's views were decidedly those of a manager. Additionally, his personal circumstances were unmistakably different from the Silicon Valley workers for whom professional moderation work was their sole and primary livelihood. Financially secure, Rick had been doing commercial content moderation work by choice, although, at the time of our interview, he was largely out of the day-to-day work of moderation and involved with management of others. His perspective is valuable not only as a manager, but as someone working for a boutique firm. His frame of reference for commercial content moderation's role in a business environment was therefore primarily predicated on the importance of a positive corporate internet presence for his clients. That perspective was the motivation informing his comments on the services that OnlineExperts offered.

Generous with his time, Rick spoke to me on Christmas Eve of 2012 via video chat from Mexico. Rick was in his home office, dressed in casual resort-style tropical leisurewear, as the sun streamed in through his window, and I sat in Wisconsin, as the snow fell and the icy wind blew outside.

Working Virtually, Working from the Cloud

Rick got his start in CCM by doing the moderation in Online-Experts' early days and later moving on to developing the corporate protocols and training processes for the firm's moderators and teams. He described in detail the various levels of the company and how the employees interacted among them and with each other. The firm's 260 employees were dispersed around the world. Although the company is based in Canada, there is no OnlineExperts physical headquarters or campus; all

work is conducted from the workers' homes or other work-
spaces of preference and facilitated by the internet. He told me,
"I started in 2008, early 2008, I was actually employee number
seven with the company. And we now have about 260. We've
grown a lot in the last four years—that's five years. I started out
moderating content in 2000 to early 2008, and as we grew, just
my management experience and all that just sort of led me to
grow with the company and take more senior positions, so I'm
certainly not retired anymore."

During his time with OnlineExperts, the firm had experienced exponential growth, a reflection not only of Rick's
business acumen and ability to attract clients, but also closely
mirroring the rise and popularity of social media platforms. As
the social media landscape transformed from users interacting
in forums and comment sections into a variety of platforms
and using a variety of media, the firm transformed with it. As
he explained,

> In 2002, that's really what [OnlineExperts was] do-
> ing, was content moderation. Over the years—and
> basically at that time we started moderating—we
> were really moderating news content for newspa-
> per websites, we were doing some video/television
> show moderation, live video broadcasts where peo-
> ple could text in their requests and comments and
> that type of a thing. In 2008 we landed our first big
> client, a media company that we started doing the
> online moderation for. That one was really the—
> no one had started doing that. There was nobody
> out there. Any moderating, newspapers were doing
> themselves. We started doing that, and that led
> to another newspaper, and that led to another,

another newspaper site, and at that time there really were no brand pages for Facebook, either, I mean, this was really in its infancy. As we started to, to grow some of these media companies and others said, "Okay, we've got a Facebook page here and we want that content moderated." That sort of branched into the moderation of Facebook pages, and then as things—you know, more recently, Google+ and Instagram and YouTube brand pages, those type of things have added to it. Now a lot of our revenue comes from actual community management, where we're the face of the brand.

Unlike the commercial content moderation workers at MegaTech, who trekked each day via MegaTech's corporate buses to their Silicon Valley campus for on-site work (with the occasional day working from home), the entire Online-Experts team was spread around the globe. There was no physical headquarters, no office, no central place that workers or teams gathered. Instead, they worked virtually and usually out of their homes, from wherever in the world they were located. Rick discussed the staffing model at OnlineExperts with me at length, describing how the company relied on a variety of commercially available internet tools to facilitate the workflow of the company's many employees. These tools were primarily publicly available and cloud- and web-based, which also meant a low technology infrastructure overhead for OnlineExperts, in addition to the cost savings effected by not having any physical locations. Rick did not seem to have any concerns about the fact that the tools and services the company was using were completely outside the control of the firm, however.

Our 260 employees have no offices. Everyone from
our CEO on down works out of their home. We
rely on those type of communication tools, we
think we've got it pretty well down to a science.
We use chat rooms for individual teams; we have
thirteen client services managers, and each of them
has a team chat room that anyone in management
can go into, but these are really for the moderators
on that team to collaborate, you know, "Heads up,
this is going on," "This site, keep an eye out for it,"
and also it's sort of a water cooler type of thing, so
they can meet and chat, let off some stress. It's not
just you sitting all by yourself in your house working; you've got a team somewhere else in the world,
or you know, in North America, or wherever you
are, that you can chat with. We use Google Talk for
individual chats back and forth. We use Google
Hangout, you can put up to ten people in there, so
team meetings often take place in Google Hangout,
or GoToMeeting, what else do we use . . . Skype, of
course. And the telephone. Those are the communication tools that we use, they're all publicly available; we have nothing proprietary there.

Although Rick saw the online platforms that he and his
team used as being "public" and "not proprietary," they were
only in the sense that OnlineExperts had not built them, did
not own them, and really did not even control them. It was not
clear what OnlineExperts might do if one of the tools they
relied on disappeared, was discontinued, or went to a fee structure that could greatly affect their bottom line. The lack of
insight about what constituted public versus private tools

was particularly curious given the fact that Rick was keen to make this distinction in other contexts: "We use Google Sites as a platform, so each of the team has their own site, and a subset of that is client sites that contain all the client-specific information. We've got a group of technology guys that have built moderation tools, so they've actually designed the tools that pull the content out of Facebook into our tool, we modify or delete the content, it deletes it off the Facebook page, and so on."

With the exception of this very minimal tool developed for OnlineExperts, the company not only avoided automation and specialized platforms to deal with its commercial content moderation and brand management functions, but actually prided itself on this aspect of the process. The lack of control over the tools they used to coordinate moderation activities and intercompany communication, as well as to deal with proprietary information that their clients likely would not want third parties to be able to access, did not seem of concern or to be a liability, in Rick's estimation. Indeed, he considered the technological leanness to be a selling point of the company's service: "That's one of the pitches that we do to our clients, is that we use human-powered moderation. We don't use robots, we don't use filters, we don't try to automate this process, we have human power, which, you know, it leads to a great deal of accuracy versus filters and tools, but it also, to err is human, so [some errors] are going to happen."

Without the same level of engineering expertise and available labor to create custom tools, OnlineExperts had managed to develop a system relying on employee mastery of particular workflow norms, as well as the ability to quickly seek out information relevant to a particular brand or product for which they were moderating. In this way, OnlineExperts put its full trust and responsibility for accurate, timely, and appropriate commercial content moderation decisions on the shoulders of its moderators as well as great trust in the availability of the platforms upon which they all relied for communication and moderation activities.

Social Media Expertise as Brand Protection

Although the firm began as a strictly commercial content moderation operation, offering its services to news and media companies challenged by the comments sections of its online properties that could quickly devolve into unusable hostile zones, the business quickly expanded into other areas of social media management as quickly as the need for it arose. OnlineExperts focused its services on companies that did not have expertise in social media and whose primary business was something other than social media or technology in general. For this reason, the firm saw an opportunity to expand its own services to meet the needs of companies that wanted a presence across many social media platforms (for example, Facebook, Twitter, Instagram) but lacked the expertise and knowledge to properly manage their brand identities in all of these spaces, particularly in the event of a crisis precipitated by a social media flare-up or unexpected reaction to a campaign. Rick described where OnlineExperts fit into a client's business model and what it provided: "That's sort of the way we identify ourselves: brand protection. More brand protection, but also brand management. And many of the brand management—we're actually hired by advertising agencies, so the agency manages the brand and, in many cases, they'll supply us with a calendar of content or, you know, they work with us to create content for specific sites."

Not only were OnlineExperts' content moderation employees responsible for monitoring and taking down problematic content that might pose a threat to a brand, but they also actually created new content, seeding sites with messages and discussion points designed to encourage customer participation and engagement, and to bring a positive face to the brand or product. All of this activity was done surreptitiously, without OnlineExperts' employees ever identifying themselves as such, instead posting under the moniker of the company or brand, or even posing as other regular, unaffiliated consumers. As Rick put it:

> We're posting on behalf of the brand. We're engaging with consumers, and so on. We still do a lot of moderation, all the sites require moderation, but it has expanded to a lot more: analysis and reporting, what is going across, what are people saying about your brand across the whole social media spectrum, and sentiment analysis, whether the comments are positive, negative. People call us in for a crisis. We've never worked with some of these clients before and suddenly somebody does something stupid at the organization and their Facebook page blows up and they call us in for a crisis. Here's a perfect example of the weirdest thing I've ever heard, but a snack food company, a year ago or so, posted a pro-LGBT image ... and within four hours they had over twenty thousand comments on their Facebook page, many homophobic rants and so on. Why people are doing that on a snack food brand's Facebook page, I have no idea, but they called us in to help manage that, and so that kind of thing goes on fairly regularly.

In such a case, OnlineExperts would be called in to manage
the ensuing mess and mitigate the damage, deleting unflattering
and hostile comments and seeding the brand's many social media
profiles with positive messages to redirect the flow of conversation. These activities would take place covertly, without a clear
indication that the postings were coming from a firm hired to
encourage positive engagement with a product or brand, or to
delete messages that detracted from that brand's identity. In this
way, OnlineExperts operated behind the scenes, steering content
and engagement to meet a particular brand's desired outcomes.
OnlineExperts was able to tailor its online brand management
to a client's own profile, develop a unique brand voice for that
client, and achieve specified outcomes as agreed upon between
the client and the firm, often along with an ad agency. This level
of attention to detail and tailoring to an individual client's needs,
as well as its ability to manage facets of the user experience and
brand identity across numerous social media platforms, is characteristic of boutique-style firms such as OnlineExperts.

Additionally, although OnlineExperts is a Canadian firm,
it has numerous large multinational clients based across North
America, and its moderators need to be able to adjust for
cultural context, as well as to each client's particular profile
and values. This was a challenging aspect to the business, as
Rick told it, and the commercial content moderation staff at
OnlineExperts needed to be adept at moving among many different profiles with different tolerances for risk and for contro-
versial content in order to match a client's profile. They also
need to be aware of issues that might shift and change based
on where a company is located in the world.

It's difficult to keep the brand voice consistent unless you create—and we do this as well—we create

templates that say, "if the poster says this, here's the canned response," but a lot of clients don't want canned responses. They want a canned response put in your own words but to still reflect the brand. Training people on what is that brand culture, what is that brand voice, and how do we change these answers into your own words but still reflect the brand ... that's an ongoing training challenge in community management. In terms of moderation of content, every site has their own set of values and moderation guidelines. Some of our moderators work on multiple brands simultaneously, and some of the news outlets are very liberal in terms of what they allow, some are very strict. It's remembering if I'm moderating a Canadian website here that's very, very strict, and on the same shift I'm also moderating [an American news site]—you need to keep that straight and as a moderator you need to know which guidelines fit which account, or have a quick reference to check each comment, versus what's allowable.

Employee Values/Corporate Needs: The Employees of OnlineExperts

Over the years, OnlineExperts' contractor profile had morphed along with the portfolio of clients and suite of services it was able to offer. Unlike MegaTech, which actively sought young, and presumably social media–savvy, recent college grads for its commercial content moderation team, OnlineExperts needed a different kind of expertise in the early days. It sought out early retirees and people older than forty to handle the news sites because the younger employees were not able to contextualize the newsworthy global events they were required to moderate. Rick told me, "When we started with the news commentary, you know, it's not a great-paying job being a moderator. It's ten bucks an hour, which is not bad ... for a home-based business, you're guaranteed hours and so on. When we started with the big news sites we hired college kids and part-timers, but we quickly found out that they were not the right people to work on news sites because, even though they were university, college [educated], they really have no historical context for what went on in the world."

Recalling how Caitlyn Brooks struggled to contextualize content for MegaTech, it is clear that Rick had identified a need and a niche, but there were still generational struggles for the company to address. Although OnlineExperts initially had to shift from younger to older moderators for newspaper website moderation, once its clients began to include social media sites, it had to shift back to younger moderators.

> Many of those people are still with us, but they are not comfortable with other social media entities. They don't use Facebook, they don't use Twitter, so as we started moderating the Facebook pages, we, our [employee] demographic changed to a younger demographic who were more comfortable using those tools and understood the context of what a Facebook post was and why, you know, why people posted on Facebook, which, I don't want to say the older generation because I'm pretty old to be in the social media space, I'm fifty-five, but I've kept up with it, whereas many people my age don't under-

stand the logic behind it or the compelling—the reason why you want to be on Facebook. So it's changed
to a younger demographic, and now that we're doing
a lot of engagement, it's changing again.

As with all the other commercial content moderation
workers I spoke with, Rick identified the need for moderators
to understand the difference between their own values and those
of their client, and to be able to compartmentalize the former
while on the job, in favor of working from the perspective of
the latter. This was a singular challenge when working in the
fast-moving newspaper and media company forums, particularly during major news events, when moderators found themselves in the proving ground of a live and heated situation that
directly challenged their moral code. Rick explained:

> The challenge is putting aside your personal phi-
> losophy, your beliefs, your creed, and moderating
> to the client's wishes. Some of the news sites might
> be pro-NRA, some might be pro–gun control, so
> you need to put aside your personal beliefs and
> moderate, not "I think that comment is appropriate
> or not appropriate," but "I have to leave it up be-
> cause the client says it's appropriate." And there are
> people who can't deal with that. They can't put
> aside their personal beliefs and philosophies and do
> a good job of moderating, because it's totally against
> their beliefs. So that's sort of a thing that you can't
> really hire and say, "Can you do that?" because
> everybody says they can do that, but it's, you know,
> will it cause them distress? We had people say they
> couldn't sleep at night, not because the belief

system, but because the comments were so horrible. Whether it's gun control, or whether it's homophobia, or in Canada, the whole Native Indian versus White people issue is a huge thing and the comments can be very racist or homophobic, and being able to put that aside at the end of your shift is critical to be a good moderator. In some ways, you can train people to do that, but in some ways you really can't. There are times where someone leaves us just because they can't deal with that content.

Rick also expressed a bias against international workers in call center/business process outsourcing and microlabor settings, much as the commercial content moderation team at MegaTech did. In Rick's case, he considered the refusal to use such labor as a point of positive market differentiation for OnlineExperts. Nevertheless, all employees were considered contractors from a tax and employment status perspective. It was unclear whether OnlineExperts offered any type of benefits to its employees; from Rick's comments and the fact that employees were located all over the world, it was likely that it did not. Hiring workers with a "contractor" status likely facilitated the company's ability to avoid the need to comply with any local (in this case, Canadian federal and provincial) labor mandates and allowed OnlineExperts to draw a labor pool from wherever it had a need, ramping up—or down—according to its business and clientele.

Well, all of our employees—they're full or part time, but they're all employees. We don't contract out [through other labor suppliers], so all of these—some of the employees are long-term contractors. We have international people; it's a Canadian-based company, but because I live in Mexico I'm considered a contractor, even though I'm an employee of the company. But we don't third-party contract out to other moderation service companies and so on. These are all people that work exclusively for us in terms of moderation companies. Some of them have other part-time jobs or full-time jobs and do this part time, but yeah, we consider them our employees.

"Sometimes the Words Get Mixed Up": Cultural and Linguistic Authenticity as Commodity

Rick cited the notion of sociocultural and linguistic authenticity of the moderators as key to the decision to not go beyond OnlineExperts' own pool of vetted content moderation contractors, particularly when employees engaged in seeding forums or online spaces with content or engaging with the public. In other words, OnlineExperts offered the services of employees who were North American or British and could slip seamlessly into the flow of conversation or social media content dominated by English-speaking American or Canadian participants. Given the often-covert participation of the OnlineExperts employees in these spaces, the ability to not draw undue attention to oneself as inauthentic or unnatural, and, thus, away from the brand message or to any aspect of the moderation activity, was a fundamental measure of success. In these contexts, a non-local turn of phrase or unnatural grammatical construction could have unveiled the engagement as that of a professional moderator and not of, say, just another fan of a snack food talking up a product. Insider linguistic and cultural knowledge therefore was a key asset that the OnlineExperts commercial content moderation staff brought to their work.[2]

> Many of our clients or prospects that we sell to, they prefer that we do the work. So, there's offshore companies that can do some of this stuff cheaper than we can, but many of [our client's] brands, in fact, most of the brands, English is the primary language. They really want people with English as a first language doing moderation, and especially when it comes to engagement in community management. Some people with English as a second language can speak and write quite well, but sometimes the words get mixed up, or the tenses get mixed up, and it comes across as inappropriate for the brand. The business decision really is that our selling point is we do this ourselves. We don't hire third parties to do this.

As OnlineExperts' client base expanded, so, too, did its need for authenticity in other cultural and linguistic contexts and competencies beyond North America and English. Their ability to provide native speakers and people familiar with cultural contexts and social norms in other parts of the world was an important feature of their suite of services. In short, the authenticity that OnlineExperts could provide had great value for its clients.

> One of our clients is [a news channel in] Saudi Arabia, so we've got a group of moderators that are in that area of the world. We also have some of them

located in Canada that are of an Arabic background that moderate that and the guidelines are very different for something compared to [an American newspaper of record] or something like that. It's those cultural sensibilities we need when we are moderating in another language. We moderate in about twenty languages altogether. We've got people spread around the world, or we've got ex-pats like myself, we've got people in Mexico that are Canadian or American, but we've also got Mexicans that Spanish is their first language. We moderate in [Spanish], so it's really interesting dealing with the different cultural sites and reading the guidelines on how things differ from country to country.

"I Just Put It Aside": Managing the Job at OnlineExperts

As a manager, Rick expressed concern over moderator well-being, but the virtual office aspect of OnlineExperts meant that, unlike the MegaTech workers, employees were never in the same place at the same time, were not able to take lunches together or meet after a shift for drinks and downtime, and did not have access to any counseling services, cursory as those may have been at MegaTech. It was a challenge, from Rick's perspective, to encourage the moderators to create a healthy distance between their work and their time off the job.

Rick's actual knowledge of the impacts of the job on his employees was somewhat limited and was based solely on his observations, and his own experiences from several years ago doing content moderation himself. He would notice workers having trouble disconnecting from time to time, and worried about it not only from an employee well-being standpoint, but because such constant engagement could lead to faltering quality in moderation for clients and to potential burnout. Rick felt that the very nature of the job—working from home, always just a few clicks or a smartphone check away, a 24/7 cycle—was a contributing factor to problems related to an inability to disengage.

> We get the same feedback from our employees, whether it's full time or part timers, "Our clients don't know how much we care about what happens on their sites." You know, it's amazing, we're of course working 24/7, there's people moderating 24/7, but many of our workers are still in our internal chat rooms. They're still on there hours after their shift is over because they want to know what's going on. People get so invested in their job that it's a challenge, too, because you're working at home. You don't necessarily get in your car and drive home and sort of put it aside. Your computer's still on.

Rick identified his own ability to compartmentalize his on-the-job experiences as one of the factors that had led to his success in commercial content moderation, a sentiment that the workers from MegaTech also shared. Yet such compartmentalizing is not something that all people are able to successfully do, and it is not clear if behavior leading to a fracturing or bifurcation of aspects of one's work experience as a moderator from that of other parts of life leads to balance or denial, or what consequences it might raise further down the road. From the interviews with the MegaTech workers, it was clear that, even when they thought they were successful in separating their work from other aspects of their private and non-work lives, they were not always capable of doing so. Additionally, Rick's relative financial and material comfort provided him with outlets for unwinding likely not available to most commercial content moderators: "The challenge really is that: maintaining concentration for your full shift, getting the guidelines right, and being able to, at the end of the day, put all of that aside and it doesn't matter what anybody wrote. When I was moderating, at the end of the day I'd jump in the pool or we'd have friends over, and they'd say, 'Oh, what happened in the news today, you've been on all day.' I have no idea. I just put it aside, whereas other people can't."

"Not for the Faint-Hearted": On the Nature of the Net and Commercial Content Moderation Intervention

It was apparent, throughout our interview, that the internet was an entirely pragmatic space in Rick's world. For him, and for OnlineExperts, it served two purposes: it existed as a site of commerce and commercial engagement for corporate entities and their brands and products, and it facilitated the work he and his firm did to support the activities of companies in engaging with the consumer public. Rick, therefore, had very little romantic attachment to the idea of social media as a site of democratic engagement, of the merit of all speech, or of all speech being of value or being equal, or any commitment to the internet as a free speech zone, in general. Instead, he saw the internet as a series of zones of commerce, in which companies were free to set terms of engagement that he and his employees would then enforce.

On many of these sites, particularly news websites, there's a lot of folks saying, "Why was my post deleted? What right do you have to delete my opinion?" But what they forget is, it's a private site. You can go around naked in your own home, but you can't go around naked in Wal-Mart. It's the same thing. You're on someone else's site and you've agreed to the terms and conditions, as everybody has to when they sign up, so there really is no free speech on commercial sites, particularly. If you want free speech, you can start your own blog and you can allow whatever happens, that would probably be true free speech. But as soon as you're on a business or commercial site where you agreed to terms and conditions, it's not free anymore. And, you know, I'm Canadian, so from a Canadian perspective, there is no free speech in the Constitution anyway. There are certain laws. There are things you can't say.

Appeals by disgruntled users to "the First Amendment," which Rick was quick to point out was a particularly American conceit and held much less sway for a Canadian such as himself, and other sorts of hue and cry over deletions or other professional and behind-the-scenes moderation activities did not persuade him in the least. Rick was clear on the goals of OnlineExperts and, by extension, those of the clients that solicited their services.

It doesn't even translate within the U.S. because even there you can't say whatever you want. You know, you can go a lot further than you can in some countries, but it's really not pure freedom, because there is some kind of censorship or there are sensibilities, maybe, that restrict that angle. You can't yell "fire" in the theater. If it were pure free speech, you could. You know, so, there are rules and guidelines in every aspect of society, just as there are on the internet, as much as some people don't like it, or don't like to admit it, or don't want to admit it.

Ultimately, Rick's view of commercial content moderation was that it was a critical function without which the internet would be largely unusable for most people. Yet he recognized the need for balance in how and when the employees of OnlineExperts chose to intervene. This balance required human sophistication and expertise to mediate; it was a sweet spot that OnlineExperts strove to locate and negotiate with their interventions. I asked him what he thought the internet would look like without content moderation.

It would be a cesspool. You know, in fact, one of our clients has—we monitor all the stories that they publish, and we monitor all those comments and there's also a section called "Forums," which basically they say on the map, "Here be dragons." You know, beware if you're gonna post on the forum, because without the moderation there's a lot of infighting. I don't think it's possible to change someone's mind by posting on the internet, so if there's political or religion or even sports teams, people get really aggressive and a lot of personal attacks. Sites that don't have moderation at all are

not a place for the faint-hearted, because they really degenerate quickly. And that's sort of the challenge of balancing moderation is: you can't just
only allow positive comments. There has to be a—
you know, the newspapers or Facebook brands,
they want people to come to their site. When you
start overly harshly moderating, they're gonna lose
readers, because if you only allow positive men-
tions of the brand, that's not realistic either. It's that
balance of, where is that line of what's appropriate,
and where does it fall to inappropriate? And it very
easily falls to inappropriate if you let something go
and don't moderate it. But where is that tipping
point of, this one's okay and that one's not?

For Rick, OnlineExperts, and the clients they serve, brand
protection trumps all other ideas of speech; indeed, the speech
they regulate has very little to do with democratic free expression,
and much more to do with client and brand engagement with
consumers. Yet, as Rick argued, what spaces on the internet today
are not, in some way, commercial? Very few, he would contend.
The internet is also a platform for surveillance and a zone of
control. It is structured as a series of highly regulated technical
protocols and processes, built on the back end of commercially
controlled data pipes, but having front ends and user-facing layers where a variety of actors—OnlineExperts among them—moderate and manipulate content to a predetermined end. In this way,
commercial content moderation is just as critical a control
mechanism as the other protocols and functions that govern data
flow online, but one that is much less known and perhaps
even less predictable. The activities of OnlineExperts and its
content manipulation involving the brand reputation of a snack

food company seem to be, at first blush, fairly innocuous, but also suggest that much more—such as the veracity and authenticity of the content users see in online social spaces—is at stake and always for sale.

The Early Days Moderating the News

Melinda Graham and I talked in person in the summer of 2012 in New York City, where she lived at the time with her partner, a digital news executive who had previously held positions with several different American national papers of record, as well as high-level positions at an internet news and content pioneer based in Silicon Valley, YouNews. Melinda's experience with commercial content moderation work had been as a contractor, working a gig forty hours per week from home, at the time in Los Angeles, for her partner's company.

A forty-something queer-identified white woman with a varied employment background in creative fields, including in the graphic design and fashion industries, Melinda came to commercial content moderation with a long history online in numerous social media venues and internet communities. She had participated actively as a volunteer moderator for the online community and personal blogging site DearDiary, where she had moderated some highly contentious and high-volume forums. It was her connection to YouNews via her partner, and her experience doing moderation on a voluntary basis, that brought her the opportunity to work full time as an hourly contractor in a paid position for YouNews on the company's digital news sites. We talked in person one evening in her comfortable New York City apartment that she shared with her partner, Kris, who was also present, as were several elderly cats.

At the time we spoke, Melinda was the furthest removed of all those I talked to from her commercial content moderation experience; her tenure at YouNews had begun in 2007 and ended in 2008. Nevertheless, several years later, she had no trouble recalling her role, and her feelings about the job, which were largely negative. She was insightful about her own personal identity and values, and the way they often put her at odds with the content she was required to screen and in which she was immersed for much of the day. She also reflected on her paid content moderation role in contrast to the work she did on a voluntary basis at DearDiary. Finally, she had strong feelings about the value of social media as a site of expression, and its impact on both other users and people who viewed the content generated in it for a living. She told me:

> Well, I was going to start going to fashion design school; I had a very successful job that I could have stayed at indefinitely. I was a graphic designer and production artist, but I don't drive, so I found myself on the bus for three to four hours a day, because that is how Los Angeles rolls. And it was impacting my spouse because she would have to, you know, drop everything in the middle of the night and come pick me up. And she was finding herself cooking all of our meals and such because I was just working all the time. And then it's kind of dangerous to take the bus at night in LA. So she was like, why don't you just do the thing you've always wanted to do anyway and just go to school? I was very lucky in that because she worked at YouNews, and there was a need for [commercial content moderation] there. And she was cognizant of

> this—they were just starting to do these deals with
> [a TV news magazine] and YouNews. I'm sure that
> without her being there I would not have been paid
> the hourly salary at the wage that I was paid. I
> would have ended up getting significantly less.

At the start of her contract with YouNews, the company
was expanding to host forums and online discussion areas
for many other brands and properties. Much like Online-
Experts, YouNews's primary concern was not facilitating
speech in these spaces but, rather, fostering engagement while
attending to brand management and protection for its own
brand and the properties with whom it had contracted. Like
OnlineExperts, YouNews asked Melinda not only to moderate
comments that other people posted, but to generate discussion and encourage participation from users by steering
conversations in a certain direction, or steering users to particular stories or forums with comments she made. She
found that aspect of the job extremely difficult, verging on the
ridiculous.

> Because I had this experience with the community
> management with DearDiary and because I have,
> like, copy editor experience as well, and arts experi-
> ence, it was presented to me as sort of a hybrid
> thing: I would be helping with protecting those
> brands, those brand relationships. . . . I only did
> comment moderation in these other branded
> properties, where they had something to lose with
> another client or another company. So yeah. It was
> presented to me as sort of a hybrid position from
> the start, but with an emphasis on the comments.

And I found that I actually ended up doing mostly comments. But I did end up doing a lot of photo uploading and viral [content generation].... I wasn't so great at the viral stuff. Like, it's hard. I couldn't go in as an actual YouNews person, I had to be all sneaky about it. I had to make all of these fake identities to go into the YouNews groups and be like, "Hey! There's this great piece on roller skating! You should go check it out!!" [laughter]

Identity, Enforcing Civility, and the Specter of Free Speech

Early in her commercial content moderation career, Melinda found herself struggling with how to enforce civility and still allow for the free flow of ideas, all while trying to protect YouNews and its commercial and advertising relationships with other properties represented in the online forums. She found this balance almost impossible to strike, particularly as the comments and content turned to expressions of racism, homophobia, sexism, and threats.

> You know, I think the number-one thing that pissed me off about being a moderator was that all I could do was delete a comment. I couldn't [directly] comment on it, I couldn't, say, redirect the conversation. You know, if I did, in frustration, finally like go in as a pseudonym and be like, "I am the moderator." What would happen is, they would always assume you were male. And they would call you a fag. And say that you were censoring them. And,

"Be a man! Man up and like come over here and tell me to a face why you are deleting my comments, bro!" You know, "Censorship, First Amendment, arghhh!" And I would be like, "This is ridiculous." And finally, in many cases I just couldn't keep up with deleting the comments and I would go on and be like "I am the comment moderator and I'm not censoring you, you are saying 'porch monkey' and 'wetback' and that's unacceptable in this forum." And then they'd figure out, 'cause I write like a girl I guess, then they would be like, "You bitch! You cunt! I'm going to rape you." It's like, you can't really win. The frustrating thing about that was the implication that you're taking away [someone's] First Amendment right. I would assume that—which I don't agree with, I think it's stupid—but I would assume that the [YouNews] upper management was like, "We don't want to get in that fight, we don't want people to think we're censoring them." But don't get me started. My head explodes when I try to think about that.

Melinda's empathy for marginalized people made the attacks levied by other users on the sites she moderated even more difficult for her to deal with, given her own strong identification with people who were subject to identity-based abuse in their daily lives. She sensed a profound hypocrisy in the way that the right to express oneself seemed always to give more power to abusive users than to those being abused, and she had a personal sense of altruism and a notion of wanting to protect more vulnerable users from those attacks. It was a responsibility that weighed heavily on her shoulders.

It was very important to weigh the freedom of
somebody to be a hater against the freedom of, say,
viewers of color or gay viewers not to be, like, trau-
matized when they go on the site. You know? How
does the right of you to say a shitty thing weigh
more than the right of someone not to, like, who
gets called "fag" all day on the street, to not come
onto an online forum and get called "fag" all over
again? Why is your right to say "fag" more valuable
than the right of this person to not hear "fag fag
fag" all of the time? Come on, dummies! You know?

In addition to the constant homophobic slurs, Melinda
identified racial epithets as a source of great consternation.
Despite word filters that automatically removed specific offensive words on the platforms and sites she moderated, users
constantly found ways around the system, using inventive methods to post banned words, or using creative permutations of
racial epithets that Melinda had to even periodically look up to
recognize. She told me, "Profanity is obviously a big one. But
even YouNews has filters for the basic stuff. You can't say 'shit.'
You can't just type out the N-word, so I didn't have to see that
too much. But people will find a way to work around it. So again,
yes, profanity, but that's where the whole 'porch monkey' and
'wetback' thing come in. Because the lists are never long enough.
Because there is unfortunately so many racial epithets that . . .
like, you just see it . . . you're just soaking in it. You know? Yuck."
Here Melinda highlighted the need for commercial con-
tent moderation to be a human process, or to at least have
significant human oversight, due to the fact that automated
tools like banned-word lists were often subject to bypass or
failure in just the way she described. But, like other Western

professional moderators, she believed that her cultural and linguistic competencies made her a more skilled worker when it came to dealing with racial and other kinds of abuse. "This is where having somebody in the Philippines doing this is deeply ineffective. Or having it automated. Because you are going to get people trying every single way to say the N-word. And they will figure out any way around the filters. You know, just throw a couple asterisks in there and you can say it. You know? I mean, in between you can still see the whole word. Tons and tons of rape jokes. And 'bitch.' And 'make me a sandwich.' "

She also noted that abuse was not limited to the more obvious use of curse words or insults, but came in subtler and more sophisticated guises, such as the invocation of biblical passages or the use of particular turns of phrase designed to insult and anger.

> The disparaging comments, even if there's no actual profanity, the comments about a lot of scripture . . . just so much scripture. It's like religion as a weapon was just so like, that's the first thing I would look for. And I don't read a lot of Bible myself, but it was always the same "You are going to hell." It was never like "Judge not." It was always, "You are going to hell, you are an abomination, you suck." I didn't tolerate that. I don't know. Someone else might think that's okay. For me, I just don't think that's acceptable. I think that's not even a passive-aggressive way of hurting people—that's pretty aggressive.

Melinda was acutely aware of her own multiple, intersectional identities, and how they clashed with what she was required to read and see as a commercial content moderator. She struggled

with the fact that her identities seemed to make her a target or
more susceptible to experiencing the attacks she was subjected to
in her role as moderator as personal, and how she felt she needed
to sublimate these aspects of herself in order to do a good job at
moderation. She talked about this throughout our interview.

> I'm queer, I'm femme, I'm an atheist, I'm pretty
> much a working-class identified woman, I'm mar-
> ried [to another woman], I'm pretty much what
> these people hate. That's my identity and as I men-
> tioned earlier, that was not necessarily a prudent
> identity to make public when you're trying to do a
> moderation job. Because they are going to automati-
> cally accuse you of liberal bias or whatever. Whereas
> if you were, the assumption is that as a straight White
> man you would be somehow more objective . . . ? I
> don't really follow that logic, but okay. . . . You know,
> that whole default category thing. If I had been able
> to have more empowerment in terms of having an
> official moderator hat, special avatar, different col-
> ored name, or whatever, I would have probably had
> to choose a very neutral thing. Like just "YouNews
> moderator." I couldn't have outed myself as even fe-
> male, let alone any of my other identities because the
> abuse you would get from that is just . . . and then
> they assume that your moderation is invalid, too.

"I Used to Call Myself a Sin-Eater"

As Melinda continued with her commercial content moderation
work for YouNews, she found herself more and more invested
in it, devoting time that was supposed to be outside of her shifts

to thinking about what might be transpiring in the absence of her moderation. She began to put in more time than her contract called for, and her mental energy was eaten up by worry and upset caused by what she experienced in the forums she moderated. Her anxiety levels increased, and she felt an ever greater responsibility to intervene to protect others, especially when the attacks she removed were along identity lines of class, race, or sexuality.

> I actually cried a lot. And I felt dirty all the time when I was doing that job. And I got pretty anxious about, you know, I was supposed to work forty hours a week, and I ended up working many more than that. Just because I couldn't. . . . You know, I'd duck out of class and like check the things cause if I was getting into it with somebody in particular I just couldn't stand that stuff to be up there. Just knowing how it was affecting me, I didn't want other people to be affected by it. I, in my personal life, have gone out of my way to limit severely contact with abhorrent people that are shitty—specifically about these identities of mine and my friends and people I care about. So actually, having to deal directly with them was really hard. It was a bit of a shock after a while. And you do get very invested in, like, I think I probably took on that protector role even more because it was a way to shield myself from really taking personally some of the stuff that was going on. I used humor a lot. I would make fun of some of the really bad comments, just because they were so awful. I never saw an uploaded photo of child porn, but there were

two incidents that I actually reported where somebody made comments about like child raping. And
it was so disturbing.

At the same time, Melinda recognized her limited ability
to effect change of any sort. It led her to feelings of frustration
and hopelessness.

Melinda Graham: I mean it's the internet. Free speech. You can
talk about raping kids all you want, as far as I can tell. [Bitter
laughter]
STR: Your recourse was to delete and report.
MG: And that's all I could do. It's a very disempowering job.
STR: Did you feel frustrated?
MG: Completely frustrated. And I used to call myself a sin-eater.
STR: A "sin-eater"?
MG: Yeah. Like I was absorbing all of this negative energy.
And, you know, I wasn't making any kind of difference
because they are just going to go say it somewhere else. If
you go to weather.com . . . weather.com . . . Literally! There
are pages and pages of people like quoting scripture about
how gays are going to die and go to hell. I mean, it's the
weather! You could post about a kitten and it would be like
"Faggot wetback porch monkey Obama's a Muslim socialist
commie scripture." And like maybe two comments of any
kind of "Oh, what a cute kitten." You know? [wry laughter]
So, I don't know, I like to tell myself that this is just a few
teenage boys sitting in their basement being antisocial but
there were so many of them. It really made me really a lot
less likely to assume the best of my fellow humans. There's a
lot of ugly out there. And it can't all be coming from just
a few people.

A figure of folklore thought to be prevalent in Wales and England, the sin-eater was seen as a purifier in that he or she would eat, through means of bread or ale passed over the corpse of a recently deceased person, that person's mortal sins. Often a poor member of the community, the sin-eater would be compensated with financial remuneration for the taking on of another's sins through this eating.[3] In this way, those who were economically precarious were more likely to ingest the sins of others. It was with this forgotten and tragic personage of British legend, and not with anyone from the tech or social media sectors, with whom Melinda strongly identified through her work as a commercial content moderator.

At this point in our conversation, Melinda's partner dipped back into the darkened living room in which we were meeting and chimed in with her own summation, based on her years online as both a user and a professional responsible for major media properties online: "If you open a hole on the internet," she observed casually while sipping a glass of wine, "it gets filled with shit."

The Nature of "Community," Online and Offline

Melinda's longtime contributions as a volunteer moderator on a variety of online sites and social media platforms gave her an interesting point of comparison for how the work of commercial content moderation differed from those other experiences. She noted her lack of agency and control in her moderation work for YouNews versus other spaces, and a lack of clear resources or sites of support or escalation for the issues she encountered. She also highlighted the nature of online community in a space like DearDiary's "Questioning Whiteness" forum, where people self-selected and where the conversations

were very tightly moderated and very clearly bounded by guidelines and rules adhered to by all participants. Indeed, Melinda
found the very notion of "community" in the context of
YouNews to be misleading and a misnomer. She viewed the site's
forums as much less of a community and much more a space
for people to enact hostility and aggression toward one another, the very antithesis of what community stood for to her.

> Well, again, because my communities that I moder-
> ate on DearDiary I had a great deal of agency over,
> they also were a self-selected community with very
> clear, very strongly worded community guidelines
> that you had to agree with. . . . And we actually
> wrestled with this, I co-moderate that group, the
> "Questioning Whiteness" [forum]. And the moder-
> ators, we all went back and forth and there was one
> guy who was pretending to be a black woman but
> was actually a middle-aged white guy. Weird shit!
> You know? We kept having to be like, "Let's amend
> this to say you can't pretend to be black if you're
> not." You know? I can't believe we had to put that in
> the guidelines, but there you go! So when stuff
> would come up we would amend our documents.
> And we had resources, so if somebody was given a
> warning we had resources that they could go look at
> to understand why they fucked up and how to not
> do it again in the future. And the community, be-
> cause it was a closed community, and most of the
> people there were on there for a very long time,
> there was a great deal of personal investment among
> the community members to ensure that stuff got
> nipped in the bud right away. Sometimes that made

it worse. But, generally, if somebody said something that was out of line, a community member would say something and then contact one of us and say, "This happened, can you get rid of it or deal with this person...." There just is so much more empowerment and agency and self-selection. I mean people were there because they choose to be in a community that was actively about White people unlearning their racism. That's very specific.

The outcome of her experiences doing moderation work for YouNews left Melinda doubtful that the online generalist forums such as the ones it provided did anything positive for the advancement of dialogue or understanding among people. In fact, she believed it had the opposite effect and found the forums and other online spaces like it worse than useless; she found them damaging.

When you have any YouNews post [on a general-interest article] about kittens, there is no self-selection, there's no investment in the community. They're just there to be shitty and say the N-word. And quote scripture at fags. You know? They don't have any personal investment in the tone being civil and a real conversation taking place. You see that a little less in places like Huffington Post, where there is some accountability. Where people's little avatar [is displayed], and you can see the comments they've made in other places. I think Shakespeare's Sister and Jezebel have an interesting self-moderating system, but those are communities where people are rewarded for good behavior and

they are discouraged from bad behavior. And you
know, you can vote down the trolls. There is nothing like that in something like YouNews. All you
can do is flag something as abusive or say you disagree with it. Like, click.

These experiences began to color her own engagement
with other people, both online and off: "I think [the job] contributed to a lot of my depression and isolation. But like in
terms of like meeting new people and like assuming that they're
not haters, I tend not to be as positive about people as I used
to be since that. You know? And it's just, I have a much more
heightened awareness when I walk around or when I meet
friends of friends that they are probably thinking terrible things
about me. If they knew my identities, they would maybe smile
and shake my hand and wish me burning in hell."

Ultimately, Melinda questioned the utility of the generalist forums and felt that they would never be put to good use
but, instead, would always attract an element of people who
desired to engage in angry, profane postings. Melinda cited their
existence as a generator of the negative content for which she
was hired to police, echoing both Josh Santos's and Rick Reilly's
insights. "I really don't think that 90 percent of people that go
in to any online forum have any intention of having a conversation. They just don't. They want to barf out whatever it is they
wanted to say. And just gleefully barf more when they're called
on their shit. I would like to think that these people aren't like
talking like that in the real world. Because if they are, I hope
there's someone running around after them with a bar of soap.
I know that's what a lot of people think and just feel comfortable saying in these forums. But I think that's how they really
think. I think there's a lot of ugly people."

Melinda's engagement as a professional moderator in online news forums resulted in a difficult paradox: either allow people to speak freely in those spaces, leading to a site filled with invective and hateful speech, off-topic comments, and useless content, or closely monitor and moderate such spaces, infringing on people's free expression but making the site usable for the majority of visitors. Clearly, Melinda erred on the side of the latter, but was frustrated by the propensity of the forums for which she performed commercial content moderation to invariably fall into the patterns of the former. In the end, Melinda's role for YouNews was one of brand protection and management, and her closing remarks to me underscored this perspective. She advocated the shuttering of such comment sites and forums on social media properties, presaging a large-scale move by numerous major online media properties such as *Popular Science,* the *Chronicle of Higher Education,* and numerous others to do just that, or to greatly overhaul the posting process by necessitating a period of review, over the next few years.[4]

Indeed, a study from the University of Wisconsin in 2014 (also referenced in a *New York Times* article about the *Popular Science* webpage shutting off comments) demonstrated that people exposed to negative comments responding to a news story were more likely to react negatively to the content of the news story itself.[5]

Melinda put it simply: "People are horrible! [laughter] Just in having this conversation with you, I'm coming back really strongly to, you know, if you have an internet property and you don't have a very good reason for a forum—don't put it there. 'Cause it's, it's dangerous and it's ugly and it doesn't do anything for your brand. And it hurts people. So don't do it."

5

"Modern Heroes"
Moderating in Manila

Commercial Content Moderation in Manila: The Dating App Datakeepers of Eastwood City

On a stifling day in Manila, in May 2015, I sat in the back of a taxi as its driver deftly swerved in and out of bumper-to-bumper traffic, weaving around small motorbikes and scooters, past the uniquely Filipino form of mass transit known as "jeepneys," through neighborhoods populated by street vendors and small shops offering household wares and hair styling. Signs on buildings advertised "no brownouts," but precarious tangles of electrical cables suggested otherwise. In the distance, above the narrow alleyways off the main street, I caught glimpses of construction cranes and glittering towers of skyscrapers on the rise. Despite the adeptness of the driver in navigating the many obstacles, I felt queasy. We made our way to an expressway. On the shoulder, I watched as a brave and committed soul flew by our car on his Cervélo road bike as our taxi ground to a halt in stifling traffic.

We had an appointment to keep with a group of strangers I had never met, in a city and culture I was largely unfamiliar with, and the likelihood of arriving on time ticked away by the second. A colleague at my workplace, herself a native of Manila, had warned me that May would be the worst time of year for someone unaccustomed to the oppressive heat of the city to visit. She was right. I felt my carefully groomed and presentable self slipping away with each rivulet of perspiration beading on

A neighborhood scene as viewed on the taxi ride to Eastwood City from Makati City, Manila, the Philippines.

my forehead and rolling down my neck. My traveling companion, Andrew Dicks, an experienced graduate student researcher, had less trouble dealing with the climate, having spent many years living and conducting research in Southeast Asia. But even he, too, was wrinkled and damp. We sat silently in the back seat, as both of us were anticipating the day's work ahead, trying to conserve our energy in the heat.

Just as I felt certain I would not be able to stand any more heat, fumes, or weaving, the driver made a series of adroit moves, turning off the highway and on to a curving drive graced with carefully groomed tropical landscaping. He pulled over, and we stepped out on a beautiful foliage-lined walkway next to a sign announcing "Eastwood City." The meeting location had been chosen by a group of young workers who labored in one of Manila's countless "business process outsourcing" centers, or call centers, as they are commonly known. Unlike typical call center staff, the people who we had traveled to see performed a specialized, distinct type of work.

Rather than answering phones, these young people were, of course, commercial content moderators. They spent their days combing through the profiles of the primarily North Americans and Europeans who used a mobile phone dating app with millions of users. From their headquarters halfway around the globe, the app developer had outsourced its moderation work to a business process outsourcing (BPO) firm in the Philippines. The Filipino content screeners sifted through information uploaded by app users and banished what under the app's posting rules was either odious, disquieting, or illegal. Their quarry was anything deemed inappropriate by the platform itself per its guidelines, which had been passed along to the contracting firm. Inappropriateness might be as mild a transgression as the insertion of a phone number or email address into a text field where it would be visible to another user, as this was a violation of rules that would allow participants to opt out of the platform and bypass its advertising and fee structure. Or it could be as serious as a reference to or even an image of child sexual abuse. The moderators had seen the full range.

During their shifts, the focus was on meeting metrics and moving quickly to review, edit, delete, resolve. The workers had just seconds to review and delete inappropriate material from user profiles. For people whose encounters with other cultures came largely via content screening, it was inevitable that some made judgments on those cultures based on the limited window that their work offered. As Sophia, one of the workers we were meeting, later told me, "It seems like all Europeans are sex maniacs and all Americans are crazy."[1]

In the moment, there was little time to ruminate on the content they were removing. That activity was saved for later, when the moderators were off the clock and coming down from the intensity of a shift while gathered together around drinks.

It was at just such a point in the day that Andrew and I had scheduled to meet with the dating app mods. We walked further into the open-air shopping promenade to our ap-pointed meeting place—a food court featuring a bustling outpost of the American restaurant chain TGI Friday's and other similar Western fast casual chains. Young Manila urban-ites crowded the tall outdoor patio tables, which were strewn with the trappings of youthful city dwellers everywhere: large-screen smartphones, cigarette packs, and IDs and proximity badges on lanyards personalized with small stuffed animals or buttons that had been casually tossed aside in a jumble, not to be needed until the following day. As we approached, more and more young people arrived, pulling up stools and joining conversations already in progress. Many had come from work in the nearby skyscrapers emblazoned with the logos of Citigroup and IBM, as well as other perhaps less familiar BPO multinationals like Convergys, Sykes, and MicroSourcing. Servers hurriedly circled the tables, rushing to take drink and appetizer orders, bringing large draft beers and colorful, umbrella-festooned cocktails to the growing throng of workers celebrating quitting time.

The sun continued on its upward trajectory across the morning sky and radiated its heat down upon us. Elsewhere, the North American business day drew to a close. All Europe was under night's dark cover. But in Manila, drinks were arriving at the end of the workday. It was 7:00 a.m.: happy hour in Eastwood City.

We eschewed the happy hour scene at the TGI Friday's and other eateries in favor of the relative tranquility of an international coffee chain. While the commercial content moderation workers we were destined to meet were just coming off their shifts in one of the nearby high rises, we were just starting our day, and the coffee was welcome.

We took our seats and waited for our interviewees to arrive, having given them rough descriptions of ourselves. Business at the café was bustling. Most everyone in line was wearing the international symbol of office workers everywhere: a proximity access card and employee badge. They were overwhelmingly young and female. At the start of each new transaction, the café employees welcomed the customers in English with "Hi, how are you?" or "Hi, what can I get for you?" before finishing the transaction in Tagalog, ending with a singsong "thank you!" once again in English. Smooth American jazz played in the background, vibes and sax the backdrop to the lively conversations taking place among clusters of office workers. Of course, as the only obvious non-local and White Westerners in the café, we knew we stood out well enough that the workers who had agreed to meet with us would find us without trouble.

They each filtered at their own pace near 7:00 (6:00 a.m. was their quitting time), joining us and exchanging greetings. The workers, who all knew each other, and had all been in touch with us prior to our meeting, had connected to us via a peer in the business process outsourcing, or BPO, community. We had been in contact with that source, who was an outspoken community leader and popular with many call center workers in the Manila area. He had forwarded our request to meet up with Manila-based professional moderators through his large network of BPO employees, and this group of five had agreed to join us. In return for their willingness to share with us, we promised to disguise their names and key features about them, including specific locations and names of where they worked and other identifying details. As with all workers who have shared their stories in this book, their names and other details should be therefore considered pseudonymous.

The BPO employees who joined us that morning were four men and one woman. Sofia de Leon was twenty-two, the youngest of the group. She was followed in age by R. M. Cortez, twenty-three, and John Ocampo, twenty-four. Clark Enriquez was twenty-six, and the eldest, Drake Pineda, was twenty-nine. Drake was also the only one who no longer lived with his parents and extended family; he was soon to be married and planning for a family of his own. The other four still lived with parents and were responsible, at least in part, for supporting their families financially. We started our conversation there, with their families' perceptions about the work they did as moderators in a BPO setting.

STR: How do your families feel about BPO work?

Drake Pineda: It's okay. It's okay with them.

Clark Enriquez: As long as you get paid.

John Ocampo: As long as you make a contribution, it's not an issue.

STR: You contribute to your family?

John Ocampo: Actually, they think if you work in the BPO industry you will have a higher-paying salary. They thought that, because it's working a white-collar job . . . call center is like white-collar job.

Each of the moderators we met with worked for the same firm: an American company I call Douglas Staffing that has its major call center operations and the majority of its employees in the Philippines. While BPO firms in the Philippines have more typically been associated with live call center telephone work, such as service calls, customer support, sales, and technical support (referred to as "voice accounts" by many BPO employees), each of these workers was engaged solely in providing commercial content moderation services to a company that Douglas Staffing had contracted with. At Douglas, the workers were assigned to a specific account: the dating app I will call LoveLink.

Sofia, in her second year as a BPO-based commercial content moderator, was the first to describe the trajectory that led her to Douglas and the LoveLink product:

I started working last year because it was my first job after graduating. I rested for three months, then I applied for a job. Actually, it's my final interview with another company, but Douglas pulled me to attend this, uh, initial interview. Then I applied for a voice account, but sadly, unfortunately, I didn't pass. Then they offered me this, uh, non-voice. I didn't have any [knowledge] about my job because it was my first time, then I passed the initial interview, then they gave me a schedule for a final interview. Then the interviewer said, "Tell me about yourself." "I know how to edit [photos], like cropping. Then the shortcut keys, they asked me what different shortcut keys I knew. Then there was a logic example, also: "Find the difference in the different photos." Then, luckily, I passed the final interview; they offered me the job offer and contract, within the day, one-day process. Then, they told me it's a dating site. I'm excited, it's a dating site, I can find a date! Then we went through, next thing, then it's actually probationary, it's actually for six months. And then we became a regular employee. Then, we became a regular employee of last year.

Twenty-four-year-old John Ocampo had been hired at the same time as Sofia, when Douglas, early in its contract, was greatly expanding its team dedicated to moderating LoveLink. Sofia described John and herself as "pioneers," in reference to their two-year tenure on the job and on LoveLink, specifically. Like Sofia, he had initially applied to be on the phones, answering calls in real time from customers primarily from North America. A recent college graduate, he had prepared for another career but changed gears and sought employment instead in the BPO industry. He described this decision as a pragmatic one based on financial opportunity and job availability: "Actually, I'm a graduate of HRM, hotel and restaurant management, but I chose to work in the BPO industry, because at that time, the BPO was a fast-moving industry here in the Philippines.

Better chance for employment and more competitive salary. So I chose to apply for the BPO industry. And I also applied for voice first, but because of the lack of knowledge about BPO I failed many times, but I did try."

Like Sofia and R. M., as well, John arrived at commercial content moderation as a sort of consolation prize for having failed the employment examination that Douglas administered to potential workers hoping to get a position on live calls. In some aspect of that process—whether their ability to think on their feet, to speak in colloquial, Americanized English, or some combination of the two—their skills were deemed insufficient, and they were relegated to the commercial content moderation work that Douglas also undertook. In the world of Filipino BPOs, or certainly at Douglas, non-voice moderation was seen as a second-tier activity.

All five employees we met with were charged with reviewing and moderating profiles on LoveLink. Each time a user of the site or app changed anything about his or her user profile, the edit would generate a ticket that would then be reviewed by a worker like those we spoke with, to approve or deny. This included the uploading or editing of photos, a change in status, or any text the user might wish to include. Because the edits need to be approved before the profile can go live, workers were under constant pressure to act quickly. But that was not the only reason for speed. The employees reported a constant sense, and threat, of metrics by which their productivity was rated. Drake Pineda described the overall metrics process, with assistance from his peers.

Drake Pineda: The metrics is all about the . . . how many tickets we process. It's like every profile, we do some filtering. There's a lot of tickets, it's like about 1,000 every day. We have a quota, it's like 150 [tickets] per hour.

Sofia de Leon: Before it was 100.

STR: Oh, they raised it.

Drake Pineda: Because of the competitor, so 150 tickets per hour, so that makes it 150 but you do it at 200 . . .

Sofia: 150 to 300 [tickets per hour].

Productivity metrics were also measured based on length of processing per ticket, which John Ocampo described: "They have a standard like, first you have to handle the tickets for thirty-two seconds. But they, because of the increase in volume, because of the production, they have to cut it for less than fifteen to ten seconds."

In other words, over the time that Douglas Staffing had employed Sofia and her colleagues working on LoveLink, the expectation for their productivity in terms of handling tickets had effectively doubled. Although they had at one time had over thirty seconds to review and evaluate a change or an edit vis-à-vis the site's policies and guidelines, that time was now halved, meaning that the result would be a doubling of the number of tickets processed—without a commensurate pay increase.

The logic offered by the management for the increased demand in their productivity was that these increases in worker productivity were required to retain "the contract." The workers and their managers were referring to Douglas Staffing's deal to undertake commercial content moderation on behalf of LoveLink; "the contract" was both the arrangement with LoveLink, in particular, as well as a reference to keeping the commercial content moderation work in the Philippines, more generally. For all of the workers we spoke to that day in Manila, the specter of the contract disappearing to a lower-bid, higher-productivity site outside the Philippines was omnipresent. As evidence of this possibility, Clark Enriquez gave us a picture of the raw employment numbers for the LoveLink team.

STR: How many colleagues do you have right now?
Clark Enriquez: Before we reached 105 [commercial content moderation employees on the LoveLink product], but now we're only 24.
STR: Oh, did you lose some?
Clark Enriquez: We lose [them] to other vendors.

This same competitor, the "other vendor" mentioned as being responsible for the increase in productivity metrics, was identified by the whole team as being of Indian origin. Whether or not this was true, it mattered that the team saw India as a primary competitor, as they were induced to work harder, faster, and for less because of the constant fear of Douglas losing its CCM contract with LoveLink to a lower, possibly Indian, BPO bid.

John Ocampo: Ultimately, our competitors [are] from India. They were, like, bargaining, so because it's not voice [but commercial content moderation work], so it's . . . they just go for Indian salary. Here in the Philippines we have a standard [of pay], so they go to the cheapest.
STR: They go to the cheapest contract, right?
John Ocampo: They are the cheapest.

The Philippines and Commercial Content Moderation as Infrastructure

The commercial content moderation workers from Metro Manila that I spoke to in the summer of 2015 were right to be concerned about India as a site of competition for BPO-based commercial content moderation work. There has been a race for the Philippines to move ahead of India as the world's call center of choice, and it achieved this goal in recent years, emerging as the BPO—or call center—capital of the world, surpassing India despite having only one-tenth of the latter's population.[2] But that position is constantly being challenged as other regions and nations compete to solicit the world's service-sector and knowledge work. To facilitate the Philippines' ranking as the world's chief offshoring/outsourcing employment center, substantial infrastructure improvements have been made, particularly since the late 1990s, to support the flow of data and information in and out of the archipelago.

Such accommodations have included significant geospatial and geopolitical reconfigurations, particularly since the 1990s. Public-private partnerships between agencies of the Filipino government, such as PEZA (the Philippine Economic Zone Authority), along with private development firms and their access to huge amounts of capital, have transformed contemporary greater Manila and areas across the Philippines into a series of special economic zones (colloquially known as "ecozones") and information technology parks: privatized islands of skyscrapers networked with fiber-optic cables, luxury shopping districts, and global headquarters of transnational firms, incongruously within a megalopolis where brownouts are commonplace.[3]

Building off the critical infrastructure turn in digital media studies, I want to provide further context for the digital labor in the Philippines (with particular emphasis on commercial content moderation) to make the connection between the Philippines as a global labor center and the infrastructure—physical, technological, political, sociocultural, and historical—that exists to support it.[4] The cases of Eastwood City, the

Philippines' first designated information technology park ecozone, owned and developed by Megaworld Corporation, and the Bonifacio Global City, or BGC, an erstwhile military base, will be explored, all contextualized by discussion of the Philippines' colonial past and its postcolonial contemporary realities.[5]

The intertwined functions of "infrastructure" at multiple levels respond to Lisa Parks and Nicole Starosielski's statement that "approaching infrastructure across different scales involves shifting away from thinking about infrastructures solely as centrally organized, large-scale technical systems and recognizing them as part of multivalent sociotechnical relations."[6] This approach opens up the analysis of "infrastructure" to include the systems traditionally invoked in these analyses (electrical, water, communications, transportation, and so on) but also the other aspects of infrastructure—in this case, policy regimes and labor—that are key to the functioning of the system as a whole and yet have often either been treated in isolation or given less attention in the context of "infrastructure."

Parks and Starosielski urge us to look to labor not in isolation but as a primary component of infrastructure's materiality: "A focus on infrastructure brings into relief the unique *materialities* of media distribution—the resources, technologies, labor, and relations that are required to shape, energize, and sustain the distribution of audiovisual signal traffic on global, national, and local scales. Infrastructures encompass hardware and software, spectacular installations and imperceptible processes, synthetic objects and human personnel, rural and urban environments."[7] Their work is consistent with that of scholars like Mél Hogan and Tamara Shepherd, who also foreground the material and environmental dimensions of technological platforms and those who labor to make them.[8] In the Philippines, the availability of legions of young, educated workers fluent or conversant, culturally and linguistically, in North American colloquial English has been one major aspect of the country's rise in BPO work emanating from the United States and Canada. But vast infrastructure developments and policy initiatives of other kinds, including historical relationships of military, economic, and cultural dominance, have also led to this flow of labor from the Global North to the Global South.

The Filipino Commercial Content Moderation Labor Context: Urbanization, Special Economic Zones, and Cyberparks

Metro Manila comprises seventeen individual cities or municipalities, each governed independently, and a population of almost thirteen million as of 2015, making it one of the most densely populated places on earth.[9] The area's growth in population and its infrastructure development over the past decades are tied directly to the country's rise as a service-sector center for much of the (primarily English-speaking) West. Its development has been uneven as major firms locate important branches and business operations there, taking advantage of an abundant, relatively inexpensive labor force already intimately familiar, through more than a century of political, military, and cultural domination by the United States, with American norms, practices, and culture.

The availability of this type of labor force goes hand-in-hand with the service-sector work being relocated to the Philippines, which calls on linguistic and cultural competencies of workers, on the one hand, and immense infrastructural requirements (such as uninterrupted electricity, the capacity for large-scale bandwidth for data transfer, and so on) created and

maintained by private industry for its own needs. These infrastructural developments are facilitated and supported by favorable governmental policy regimes that offer immense incentive
to developers and corporations alike. Urban planning scholar
Gavin Shatkin describes the case:

> One defining characteristic of contemporary urban
> development [in Metro Manila] is the unprece-
> dented privatization of urban and regional plan-
> ning. A handful of large property developers have
> assumed new planning powers and have developed
> visions for metro-scale development in the wake of
> the retreat of government from city building and
> the consequent deterioration of the urban environ-
> ment. They have developed geographically "diver-
> sified" portfolios of integrated urban megaprojects,
> and play a growing role in mass transit and other
> infrastructures that connect these developments to
> the city and region. This form of urban develop-
> ment reflects the imperative of the private sector to
> seek opportunities for profit by cutting through
> the congested and decaying spaces of the "public
> city" to allow for the freer flow of people and capi-
> tal, and to implant spaces for new forms of produc-
> tion and consumption into the urban fabric. I
> therefore term this "bypass-implant urbanism."[10]

Although a World Bank report from 2016 on East Asia's urban
transformation stated that "urbanization is a key process in ending extreme poverty and boosting shared prosperity," the process
under way in Metro Manila reflects an unevenness, fragmenta-
tion, and expropriation of infrastructure and resources that

appear to be in the process of undergirding the stratification of and disparity in wealth and property distribution in that region.[11] According to Shatkin, the case of Manila "is not merely a consequence of the blind adoption of 'Western' planning models," but something more complex and particular to "the incentives, constraints, and opportunities presented by the globalization of the Philippine economy, which has fostered a state of perpetual fiscal and political crisis in government while also creating new economic opportunity in Metro Manila."[12]

The urbanization process of interest to Shatkin, as well as the new economic opportunity for a handful of developers and for global capital, can be linked directly to the governmental policy regimes and bodies that have administered these policies. Over the past four decades, a desire to move the Philippines onto the increasingly globalized stage for certain industries by attracting transnational corporations through favorable policies has led to an increasing reliance on private industry for investment in that development. The Export Processing Zone Authority, or EPZA, was the first agency to establish modern economic zones, the first of which was in Bataan 1969. It functioned under

> the traditional model where [such zones] are essentially enclaves outside of the country's "normal customs territory" with production of locator firms being meant almost entirely for the export market and with their intermediate and capital inputs being allowed to come in free of duty and exchange controls. To encourage investment, the zones were aimed at providing better on-site and off-site infrastructure, and locators were also granted fiscal incentives. As in other countries, the EPZs were created with the

following objectives: (i) to promote exports, (ii) to create employment, and (iii) to encourage investments, particularly foreign investments.[13]

From the development of these first export processing zones in the late 1960s through 1994, a total of sixteen such zones were established throughout the archipelago.[14] Republic Act 7916, otherwise known as the Special Economic Zone Act of 1995, paved the way for a new body, the Philippine Economic Zone Authority (PEZA), to take over the functions of the former Export Processing Zone Authority (EPZA) in 1995. This investment promotion agency is attached to the Philippine Department of Trade and Industry. The greatest shift from the EPZA's first-wave model to PEZA's second generation was the transferring of the development of the ecozones from the government to private concerns: "The State recognizes the indispensable role of the private sector, encourages private enterprise, and provides incentives to needed investments."[15]

There are special economic zones, or ecozones, for tourism, medical tourism, and manufacturing, in addition to information technology. The information technology sector was created through legislation in 1995. Megaworld Corporation, founded by Chinese-Filipino billionaire Andrew Tan in 1989, developed Eastwood City Cyberpark, and in 1999 it became the first IT park in the Philippines to be designated a PEZA special economic zone, via Proclamation 191.[16] As described on Megaworld's website:

> Eastwood City is a mixed-use project on approximately 18 hectares of land in Quezon City, Metro Manila that integrates corporate, residential, education/training, leisure and entertainment compo-

nents. In response to growing demand for office
space with infrastructure capable of supporting
IT-based operations such as high-speed telecommunications facilities, 24-hour uninterruptible
power supply and computer security, the Company
launched the Eastwood City Cyberpark, the Philippines' first IT park, within Eastwood City in 1997.
The Eastwood City Cyberpark includes the headquarters of IBM Philippines and Citibank's credit
card and data center operations as anchor tenants.
In connection with the development of the Cyberpark, the Company was instrumental in working
with the Philippine Government to obtain the first
PEZA-designated special economic zone status for
an IT park in 1999. A PEZA special economic zone
designation confers certain tax incentives such as
an income tax holiday of four to six years and other
tax exemptions upon businesses that are located
within the zone. The planning of Eastwood City
adopts an integrated approach to urban planning,
with an emphasis on the development of the
Eastwood City Cyberpark to provide offices with
the infrastructure such as high-speed telecommunications and 24-hour uninterrupted power supply
to support BPO and other technology-driven businesses, and to provide education/training, restaurants, leisure and retail facilities and residences to
complement Eastwood City Cyberpark.[17]

In other words, these ecozones operate with special dis-
pensation from taxation, more favorable rules on business
practices, such as importing and exporting of goods, as well as

with a highly developed and typically totally privatized infra-structure, separate from what is available in other areas of Manila and greatly improved. They are frequently the location for the global or regional headquarters of transnational firms that rely on both the infrastructure and the local labor market that flows in and out of the ecozone each day.

Finally, these ecozones provide housing, shopping, and entertainment for those who can afford the steep prices charged for the real estate and lifestyle they offer their denizens.

The workers themselves who circulate in and out of the cyberparks and ecozones are not typically able to partake in all of their splendor. The commercial content moderation workers we spoke to earned roughly four hundred dollars a month, and were responsible for supporting their families, in part, on that income. The workers described this rate of pay as less than one might earn on a comparable voice account, in which agents would be taking live calls in a call center rather than adjudicating user-generated content. Yet the salaries they were earning at Douglas, working on LoveLink, were ones they con-sidered on the high end for commercial content moderation work alone.

John Ocampo: We're just looking for the salary, cause for a
    non-voice account [what Douglas pays is] pretty big.
STR: Is a non-voice account usually less than a voice account?
John Ocampo: Yes, a bit less . . .
Drake Pineda: It depends on the account.
STR: And does it depend on the company too?
Sofia de Leon: Yes.
STR: Can you give us any idea of what that might be?
John Ocampo: It's around 20,000 [Philippine pesos per month]
    . . . below.

Andrew Dicks: And voice account would be?

Drake Pineda: Sometimes like a 1,000 [Philippine pesos per month] difference.

Of the five workers we spoke to, Drake was in the best position to attest to this difference in pay: he had come to commercial content moderation work at Douglas after several years of having been on BPO voice contracts. He had suffered what he described as "burnout" after years of fielding hostile and abusive calls from American customers, often angry at the fact that they were speaking to someone with a non–North American accent. Taking the pay cut to be off the phones was a bargain he was willing to make.

Bonifacio Global City

Several scholars have identified the impact of neoliberal economic planning on urban infrastructure development, and on that of the Philippines in particular.[18] Some of these cases are examples of entire cities and urban spaces being created out of whole cloth to attract and serve global economic concerns, with emphasis on the infrastructure needs of transnational corporations running on a 24/7 global cycle. Further, Parks and Starosielski have described "how an established node can be used to generate new markets and economic potentials."[19] Today's Bonifacio Global City, or BGC, in Manila is one such case.

The military encampment formerly known as Fort Bonifacio, used in succession by the Spanish and American colonial occupiers, was given over to the Philippine military before being transformed, more recently and seamlessly, into another "global city." A website dedicated to business development in the BGC waxes poetic about the transformation.

Bonifacio Global City was once part of a multi-hectare portion of Taguig that the United States government acquired in 1902 and operated as a military base. Christened Fort McKinley after U.S. President William McKinley, it was the headquarters of the Philippine Scouts, the Philippine Division of the United States Army. In 1949, three years after the Philippines gained political independence from the United States, Fort McKinley was turned over to the Philippine government. In 1957, it was made the permanent headquarters of the Philippine Army and renamed Fort Bonifacio after Andres Bonifacio, the Father of the Philippine Revolution against Spain. In the 1990s approximately 240-hectares of Fort Bonifacio was turned over to the Bases Conversion Development Authority (BCDA) to facilitate the conversion of former U.S. military bases and Metro Manila camps into productive civilian use. By 2003, Ayala Land, Inc. and Evergreen Holdings, Inc. entered into a landmark partnership with BCDA to help shape and develop Bonifacio Global City—an area once synonymous with war and aggression—into the amiable, nurturing, world-class business and residential center it is today.[20]

Today BGC is home to numerous multinational business headquarters, retail outlets, and entertainment and dining locations. It is upscale, glittering, and always under construction. It is also the site of several BPO firms involved in the commercial content moderation industry, including the headquarters of MicroSourcing, the BPO firm we met earlier offering "virtual

A street corner in Bonifacio Global City in May 2015; a Mini auto dealership is on the street-level corner, and several offices of BPOs, including those engaged in commercial content moderation and serving clients from around the world, are nearby.

captives" available to provide a ready-made and easily disassembled labor force of commercial content moderation specialists comfortable with colloquial American English, as their North American clients require.

In Metro Manila, the new and large urban development projects, such as Eastwood City and BGC, attract labor from the impoverished rural peripheries, and these workers in turn create new urban markets for labor, goods, and services, generating a need for more infrastructure and resulting in more uneven development. A new self-contained development, such as Eastwood City, may appear to have its infrastructure needs met, yet the surrounding ripple effect of lack of development often means that areas adjacent to the glimmering ecozones suffer from an acute lack of infrastructure, including power brownouts and inadequate grid support, a paucity of housing and street space, and so on.

But it is not even just the tangible disruptions at play when a location gives itself over to a development and business cycle dictated by nations and economies far afield. Labor scholar Ursula Huws describes what happens to cities and their populations under such demands: "The traditional diurnal rhythms of life are disrupted by requirements to respond to global demands. The interpenetration of time zones leads inexorably to the development of a 24-hour economy as people who are forced to work nontraditional hours then need to satisfy their needs as consumers during abnormal times, which in turn obliges another group to be on duty to provide these services, ratcheting up a process whereby opening hours are slowly extended right across the economy, and with them the expectation that it is normal for everything to be always open."[21]

Such is absolutely the case with Metro Manila's ecozones and the areas surrounding them built up, now, to support them.

The happy hours at 7:00 a.m. are emblematic of a real-life day-for-night in which the prime economic engine of the BPO firms come online once the sun has gone down, and the rest of the city, and a nation, follows suit.

Postcolonial Legacies, BPOs, and the Philippines

In her doctoral dissertation on the Filipino BPO industry, Jan Padios in 2012 described the shift of customer service call centers from the Global North to the Global South, and to the Philippines in particular, as a process predicated fundamentally on historical colonial domination of the Philippines by the United States and a continued economic and cultural relationship of dominance in the era since U.S. official political control has ended. Her book *A Nation on the Line: Call Centers as Postcolonial Predicaments in the Philippines* is an important update to this work.[22]

Padios writes, "Filipinos have been 'socialized' to speak American English and cultivate affinity for American culture as a result of U.S. occupation of the Philippines and its postcolonial legacy. . . . Many Filipinos have, in other words, developed an *intimacy with America*—an intimacy fraught with much tension and abjection—this is constructed as the cultural value that Filipinos bring to call center work."[23] Padios furthers her theoretical framing of what she describes as "productive intimacy": "Productive intimacy is the form that close relationships take when they are made productive for capital; when used as a form of corporate biopower, productive intimacy allows capital to govern workers from within their relationships, putting their affective attachments to use in the creation of exchange value and surplus value."[24] It is this interpersonal and intercultural intimacy upon which the transnational BPO market, and particularly those firms offering commercial content moderation, seek to capitalize by monetizing Filipino people's proximity to American culture, largely due to decades of military and economic domination, and selling it as a service. The evidence is in the ad copy of MicroSourcing's solicitations, but MicroSourcing is far from the only firm that sells Filipino labor to Western markets in this way.

Indeed, this value-added aspect of the Filipino BPO for the North American commercial content moderation market is well understood; doing moderation work outside one's spoken language of choice and everyday cultural context is extremely difficult and presents novel and distinct challenges, so any mechanism that provides increased skill (or perception thereof) in these areas can be operationalized by firms in the industry. As John Ocampo confided, "Before [doing professional moderation work] we didn't have any idea about [American] racial slurs." Yet the Douglas contractors for LoveLink had become quick studies in the array of racial denigration that its North American users might employ in their dating profiles, and, after all, they had the internet and its vast tools to use when deciding whether to allow a particular turn of phrase in a user profile or not. "Actually," Clark Enriquez exclaimed, when encountering potentially racist insults or descriptions, "we can go to Urban Dictionary" to look them up. "Sometimes," Andrew and I confessed, "we have to do that, too."

For the Western firms in need of commercial content moderation work who choose to outsource, there is an additional appeal. Just as in the textile and manufacturing sectors (such as Apple contracting with Foxconn, or H&M with various contract textile manufacturers in Bangladesh), creating layers of contractors between the firm where the work originates and the ones that actually carry it out lends plausible deniability when there are repercussions for this work. When a commercial content moderation worker finds himself distraught over the uploaded content he views every day in his employment, he is typically precluded by geography, jurisdiction, and bureaucratic organization from taking any complaints directly to Facebook, Google, Microsoft, or any of the major tech or social media firms his work ultimately benefits. In utilizing offshore contracting firms, companies that outsource their commercial content moderation put it, quite simply, out of sight and out of mind. Although the workers we met supported LoveLink's product and, by extension, the company that owned it, it was unlikely that anyone at LoveLink would think of the people doing moderation at Douglas Staffing as their employees, if they thought of them at all. Indeed, that disconnect and uneven dynamic was by design.

At the turn of the millennium, sociologist Manuel Castells famously theorized the "Network Society," an information-driven economy characterized by the compression of time and space into a "space of flows" and organization and labor practices reconstituted into flexible, reconfigurable, and dynamic structures that more closely resembled interconnected nodes than they did the top-down hierarchies of the factories and plants of the industrial era.[25] Such organization, enhanced by the digitized, data-driven computational power of global informational connectivity, transcended geospatial boundaries into global networking arrangements and was no longer limited to a traditional work day, but could function across time zones and around the clock. Yet this seeming rupture with traditional hierarchies and relationships has not proved to be as radical or liberatory as portended almost thirty years ago, as it has been taken up in the service of other political and economic ideologies. Instead, we see acceleration and flexibility of work and

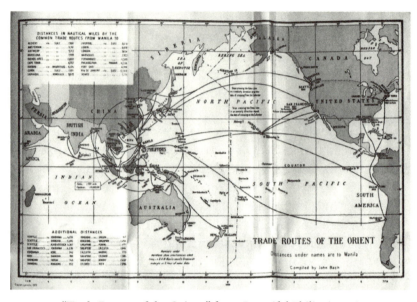

"Trade Routes of the Orient," from *Beautiful Philippines: A Handbook of General Information*, 1923. (Courtesy of the Newberry Library)

worksites, a phenomenon many scholars, such as David Harvey, decry as quintessentially neoliberal in nature, of benefit almost solely to employers and corporate interests.[26] And the trajectory of the "flow" looks very similar to well-worn circuits established during periods of formal colonial domination and continuing now, via mechanisms and processes that reify those circuits through economic, rather than political or military, means.

"Eastwood City's Modern Heroes"

After our meeting with the five Douglas Staffing commercial content moderators, Andrew and I decided to explore the Eastwood City information technology park a bit more on our own. We saw many North American and international chains, such as the Coffee Bean & Tea Leaf and the Japanese fast-fashion store Uniqlo, among the gardens, fountains, and walkways of the ecozone. We wandered through the open-air mall as workers hosed down the foliage and repaired the tiles of the plazas and pathways. As the early morning hours ceded to a more reasonable time for families and older people not on the BPO clock to make their way into the area for shopping or dining, the plazas began to fill up with people meandering through the space in large, intergenerational family groups or in smaller groups of young people together, often arm-in-arm, shopping bags in tow.

Despite having never been to Eastwood City before, I was seeking out one particular feature. I was aware that there was a statue placed there, a sort of manifestation of banal corporate art that most people probably did not pay a great deal of attention to under ordinary circumstances. The statue, I understood, was dedicated to the workers who labored in the BPO sector. I was hoping to see it for myself.

As we walked in the direction that I made my best guess it might be in, Sofia and John came striding up. They had decided to stay at Eastwood City after our interview and do some sightseeing of their own. Where were we headed, they asked? When I described to them the statue I was seeking, they knew immediately what I was talking about, and invited us to follow them directly to it.

The statue was one of many elaborate corporate artwork installations that decorated the ecozone. Some were fountains decorated with a variety of motifs and ornate; others were lifelike bronzes of family dogs. But this one was special—quite large, with a round pedestal that filled up a central portion of the plaza where it stood. On its base was a plaque that read:

> This sculpture is dedicated to the men and women
> that have found purpose and passion in the busi-
> ness process outsourcing industry. Their commit-
> ment to service is the lifeblood of Eastwood City,
> the birthplace of BPO in the Philippines. Eastwood
> City was declared under Presidential Proclamation
> No. 191 as the Philippines' first special economic
> zone dedicated to information technology. EAST-
> WOOD CITY'S MODERN HEROES

I stood in front of the looming statue, endeavoring to
capture it from several angles, so that the different people it
represented—a woman seated at a desk, a man carrying a brief-
case and a book and in a dynamic pose, another woman also
seemingly frozen in movement, with a ledger under her arm—
all would be featured in one photo or the other. The statue was
large enough so that getting each figure in detail was difficult
without the multiple shots. I noticed while I was going through
my photo shoot that some of the shoppers and visitors to Eastwood City, as well as the crew replacing tile nearby, seemed to
notice my interest in the statue and found it odd, as if to say,
"You know that's just cheesy corporate art, right?" or perhaps,
"We have art museums in Manila if you want to go there to
check them out." It made me self-conscious, as it probably
seemed silly to give so much attention to what most would walk
right past.

The statue towered over the plaza, three figures, oversized
and fashioned out of metal in business casual attire. Each of
the three figures of the statue was faceless, Eastwood City's
everyman and everywoman, but, importantly, each one wore a
headset signifying his or her role as a voice on the other end of
the line. The reference to "modern heroes," too, was important:

A statue in Eastwood City, Manila, commemorating the
Philippines' BPO workers, which it describes as "modern heroes."

the Filipinos who had left the archipelago to work abroad
throughout the twentieth and twenty-first centuries—
collectively known as Overseas Filipino Workers, or OFW—
were often referred to by the Filipino government and media
as "new heroes." Here were the modern ones who could now
work abroad while staying at home—from the call center.[27] The
statue needed some updating, I thought, to represent the
newer labor forms taking hold in the BPOs in Eastwood City
and in other areas throughout Manila just like it. But how would
an artist depict the work of commercial content moderation?
The statues would likely be faceless, just like these, but no
headsets would be needed. The work was cognitive—purely
mental—and the challenge to the artist would be to depict the
trajectory from the moderator's mind to the action of a click
to delete or skip. Perhaps, even more difficult, the artist would

have to find a way to demonstrate absence in a bronze. Would they depict the excessive drinking? Could they find a way to show the moderator insulating herself from friends and family? Or suffering a flashback from an image seen on the job? For now, the traditional phone workers and voice account representatives of the BPOs would have to suffice as stand-ins.

After I got my photos of the statue, Sofia and John surprised me by asking for a favor. Each one handed me a Samsung smartphone and asked me to take a snapshot of them together as they stood in front of the statue. They smiled into the camera as I pointed, clicked, and heard the electronic reproduction of a camera shutter. In this way, even for just a moment, commercial content moderators were represented alongside the better known BPO workers present in the plaza. We said our goodbyes after that and went our separate ways, the two of them flowing back into the growing crowds of shoppers and passersby until they disappeared completely from our view.

6

Digital Humanity

"You know, I've had conversations with people about my research and my interest in the topic," I told Max Breen, "and they say things . . . like, 'Well, why don't you just go get one of those jobs and document what it's like?' "

Max replied: "Don't put yourself through it."

Summer 2018, Los Angeles, California

Commercial content moderation, the human adjudication of online user-generated social media, is work that often occurs in secret and typically for relatively low wages. When I began my research in 2010, there was little language to describe professional moderation, locate where moderation happens in industrial contexts, or even identify who did the moderating. Understanding this phenomenon, giving voice to the workers who undertake it and situating it in its industrial context—among the firms that need these services and those that provide them—has become my life's work, in no small part because it has become clear to me that understanding moderation and the people who moderate is crucial for understanding the internet as we know it today. Over the past eight years, during which I have tracked these practices, met workers, and written about the moderators and the work they do in a variety of academic and public outlets, commercial content moderation as a fundamental facet of the commercial social internet has gained in prominence in the public consciousness and, increasingly, in the eye of legislators and regulators around the world.[1] In part, this is because academic researchers or investigators interested in the social impact of the internet have made this a concentrated area of study, often with little support and sometimes with active hostility from both industry and academia. Thankfully, this is now changing.

Key partners in bringing commercial content moderation to light have been the journalists covering Facebook, Google, and other firms, reporting on Silicon Valley, or responsible for similar beats related to social media. Some of them have published significant exposés that have had a deep impact: throughout 2014 I had lengthy conversations with the journalist Adrian Chen, who had covered some early commercial content moderation stories while at Gawker and was then writing a major feature for *Wired* magazine. His resulting article was the impetus for many people to consider, for the first time, the actions of social media companies in content gatekeeping, and the legions of commercial content moderation workers dispersed globally in places like the Philippines, where he traveled for the story. Chen's article continues to circulate today as a prime and early description in the popular press of commercial content moderation and its implications.[2]

Other reporters have followed suit, and the work they have done has been powerful: Olivia Solon and Jamie Grierson's "Facebook Files" for *The Guardian* in 2017, Julia Angwin's coverage of content moderation for ProPublica in 2017, Catherine

Buni and Soraya Chemaly's exposure on the "Secret Rules of the Internet" for *The Verge* in 2016, or the German case of content moderation reported by Till Krause and Hannes Grassegger in the *Süddeutsche Zeitung,* in 2016, are a few important examples.[3] The pressure from journalists has resulted in forcing responses from social media firms that has made it no longer possible for them to deny the existence of commercial content moderation workers as a mission-critical part of the social media production chain. Indeed, as scandal after scandal unfolded in online social spaces (murders streamed over Facebook video functions; the availability of disturbing content featuring or targeting children on YouTube; the eruption of concern over the existence of fake news on all platforms and its influence on electorates in various parts of the world), the moderators themselves were often invoked by the firms that employ them as the solution to the problems.

It was due to this pressure that we learned, for example, that Google planned to take its staffing to twenty thousand commercial content moderation workers dealing with a variety of its products and problems, and Facebook was acknowledging plans for half as many.[4] This stance represented a stark about-face from the past, when queries about commercial content moderation practiced at the platforms were met with silence or treated lightly by corporate spokespeople (such as Microsoft's "yucky job" quip to NPR's Rebecca Hersher in 2013). Now, it seemed, professional moderators were the front line of brand and user protection, although still, next to nothing was being said about the nature of the work and how the hiring would be undertaken. My sense was that the vast majority of those workers would be hired worldwide and that third-party contracting firms would likely be used to staff in-house and call center mods. After all, shoring up a workforce of this size so quickly would be difficult to impossible without using a global labor pool to provide the cultural and linguistic competencies needed for a worldwide audience at the bargain-rate prices that would appeal to the firms.

In the past few years, the public's distrust and questioning of the impact of commercial social media platforms on all aspects of their lives have grown. This has come in the wake of many scandals like those I described earlier, but also in light of the unexpected political triumph of Donald Trump in the United States in 2016, and of the Brexit campaign in the United Kingdom in the same year. As scholars and analysts continue to pick apart the mechanisms by which these political turns were influenced by online disinformation campaigns (such as the Cambridge Analytica scandal of 2018, as one example), the public and, increasingly, legislators have begun to ask more sophisticated questions about how their social media ecosystem is made. In any such discussion, I argue, accounting for the internet's for-pay gatekeepers, commercial content moderators, must take place.

To that end, I have responded to numerous requests for media interviews, appeared as a guest on radio and television programs, and lectured extensively on commercial content moderation workers and their work. Far from the cloistered and lonely research of my early years, I have found a number of communities also committed to defining and drawing attention to these practices, sometimes for different ends, but all in overlapping ways. These include individuals involved in civil society advocacy; those concerned with internet freedom issues; people committed to freedom of expression and human rights, writ large; people concerned about worker well-being; legal scholars interested in internet jurisdictional, governance, privacy, and procedural issues; scholars who look at the future and the nature of work; researchers committed to the fostering of a healthier internet for all—the list goes on. I am indebted to these colleagues, whom I consider a community of practice for my own research and, indeed, the members of a nascent sort of content moderation studies.

Evidence of this coalescence can be found in many places, including in my convening of a first-of-its-kind open-to-the-public conference at UCLA in December 2017 that saw the participation of some one hundred people—academics, activists, students, journalists, and professional commercial content moderation workers among them—engaged in various ways with content moderation in its many forms. The participants and presenters at this conference, titled "All Things in Moderation," included the United Nations special rapporteur on the promotion and protection of the right to freedom of opinion and expression David Kaye; attorney Rebecca Roe, who represents a commercial content moderation worker suing his employer for disability after ten years on the job; a panel of journalists who cover the commercial content moderation beat in some way; and perhaps most powerfully, Roz Bowden and Rochelle LaPlante, two women who have worked in the past and currently work as commercial content moderators, respectively.[5]

Since then, several other conferences and events focusing on content moderation policy and practice have taken place, including the "Content Moderation at Scale" event at Santa Clara University in February 2018, one in Washington, D.C., in May 2018, and another in New York City in late 2018.[6] Numerous conversations about commercial content moderation are taking place at academic and tech conferences and congresses held throughout the world, with tangible policy outcomes just beginning to be the result. I anticipate much more to come.

Indeed, one industry insider who requested anonymity told me in the summer of 2017 that his firm considered commercial content moderation "a one-billion-dollar problem." I then knew we were only at the beginning of a long-term and major conversation.

Today, the stakes for social media firms are much higher than ever before, and online life can and does frequently have real-world offline impacts that are a matter of life and death. As just one bleak and disturbing example, the ongoing discrimination and violence toward the Rohingya minority of Burma (also known as Myanmar) has been stoked by online hate campaigns primarily conducted on Facebook. These online expressions of ethnic feuding have resulted in violent mob killings, leading many of the Rohingya to flee into exile in neighboring countries like Bangladesh, and may have been organized by the Myanmar government in a concerted effort of media manipulation to the end of consolidation of political power. Can commercial content moderation, undertaken on behalf of the world's largest social media firms, be an effective bulwark against such manipulation, exploitation, and propaganda with deadly outcomes, or is it simply part of a larger enterprise—a social media industry based on user-generated content at all costs—that ultimately facilitates it? As just one example, it may well be that the power and allure of using such channels unprecedented in their scope and ability to be exploited is simply too irresistible for state actors, among other parties eager to orchestrate and engage the platforms' capabilities to undisclosed propagandistic and other potentially even more nefarious ends.[7]

Facebook's head of Global Policy Management, Monika Bickert, was unusually candid about the challenges facing her company's platform when she spoke at the conference held at Santa Clara University in February 2018, as reported by Alexis

Madrigal in the *Atlantic*. Madrigal noted that "the content moderation challenge is different from the many competitive bouts and platform shifts that the company has proven able to overcome. It's not a primarily technical challenge that can be solved by throwing legions of engineers at the problem." Indeed, despite Facebook's vast wealth in both monetary and technical terms, Bickert acknowledged that many of the problems facing Facebook's content teams are unlikely to be quickly or easily solved in the near term. And as for artificial intelligence, Madrigal reported Bickert's unequivocal response. "That's a question we get asked a lot: When is AI going to save us all? We're a long way from that."[8]

What this means in the near- and even mid-term is that companies that require social media gatekeeping of user uploads will continue to turn to human beings to fulfill that need. This means that the global workforce of people who perform social media moderation as a professional, for-pay task as either part-time or full-time work will increase. And just as it has at Google and Facebook, the workforce will increase across all the sectors where commercial content moderation takes place, from the boutique in the cloud to the digital piecework microtasks on Amazon Mechanical Turk. Researchers, engineers, and social media firms themselves will assuredly continue to develop artificial intelligence tools to ease the burden of moderation and to contend with the volume of content uploaded. The widescale adoption of PhotoDNA, an automated tool that uses algorithms to find and remove child sexual exploitation material that has been recirculated on social media sites, across the social media industry portends the use of such automation that could be applied in other cases.[9] But such material must already be included in a database of identified bad content in order for it to be successfully removed by automated means.

Further, identifying what constitutes child sexual exploitation material may be a relatively straightforward, albeit grim, process, but the issue becomes a thorny and complex problem when applied to other types of automated moderation and removal. Consider the eGlyph project, based on the same technology of hashing algorithms as PhotoDNA, but targeting "terroristic" content instead.[10] Who will program these tools to seek out terroristic material? By whose definition? And how will users ever know when they are being deployed and on what terms? To be sure, an algorithm is much less likely to be responsive to meaningful or routine oversight, much less to leak to the media or be interviewed by academic researchers, than a human moderator. Indeed, this may be an incentive not lost on the firms and policy makers that seek to replace human screeners with artificial intelligence–based computational tools. To be sure, without the willingness of human moderators to talk to me, in violation of nondisclosure agreements and employment contracts in almost every case, this book could not have been written.

Ultimately, even the significant advancements in artificial intelligence automation fall short of current demand and remain primarily aspirational. One obvious solution might seem to be to limit the amount of user-generated content being solicited by social media platforms and others, but this is an option that no one ever seems to seriously consider, a point noted by Dartmouth computer scientist and PhotoDNA creator Hany Farid in his paper on the tool's uptake.[11] The content is just too valuable a commodity to the platforms; it is the bait that lures users in and keeps them coming back for updates to scroll, new pictures or videos to view, new posts to read, and new advertisements to be served.

So commercial content moderation will therefore continue to fall to legions of human beings worldwide. They will be

asked to make increasingly sophisticated decisions and will often
be asked to do so under challenging productivity metrics that
demand speed, accuracy, and resiliency of spirit, even when
confronted by some of humanity's worst expressions of itself. As
Max Breen said so poignantly and concisely of the work he and
tens of thousands of others do: "It's permanently damaging." The
effects of that damage can be even more powerful when workers
report an inability to sufficiently separate the responsibilities of
their jobs from their time off the clock, whether it was sufficiently divorcing their sense of protecting users from seeing or
experiencing harm, or the phenomenon of something disturbing
from their workday invading their psyche when at home.

At this time, there are no publicly available short-term or
longitudinal studies concerning the effects of commercial content moderation on the workers who do it. It is possible that
some companies that rely on these practices have done internal
psychological assessments or have otherwise tracked their employees' mental and physical health and well-being, but if they
have been completed, the studies are assuredly highly guarded.
Without this information, the development of effective wellness
and resilience plans for commercial content moderation workers across the industry by qualified mental health and other
professionals is difficult. That said, some members of the tech
and social media industries have banded together into the
benignly named "Technology Coalition," ostensibly to focus on
these issues.[12] The firms listed as members of the Coalition as
of late 2017 were Adobe, Apple, Dropbox, Facebook, GoDaddy,
Google, Kik, LinkedIn, Microsoft, Oath, PayPal, Snap, Twitter,
and Yahoo. As I wrote for *Techdirt* in early 2018:

> Several major industry leaders have come together
> to form the self-funded "Technology Coalition,"

whose major project relates to fighting child
sexual exploitation online. In addition to this key
work, they have produced the "Employee Resilience Guidebook," now in a second version, intended to support workers who are exposed to child
sexual exploitation material. It includes information on mandatory reporting and legal obligations
(mostly US-focused) around the encountering of
said material, but also provides important information about how to support employees who can
be reasonably expected to contend emotionally
with the impact of their exposure. Key to the rec-
ommendations is beginning the process of building a resilient employee at the point of hiring. It
also draws heavily from information from the
National Center for Missing and Exploited Children (NCMEC), whose expertise in this area is
built upon years of working with and supporting
law enforcement personnel and their own staff.[13]

The *Employee Resilience Guidebook* is a start toward the
formation of industry-wide best practices, but in its current
implementation it focuses narrowly on the specifics of child
sexual exploitation material and does not appear to be intended to serve the broader needs of a generalist commercial
content moderation worker and the range of material for which
he or she may need support.[14]

Unlike members of law enforcement, who can invoke and
lean on their own professional identities and social capital for
much-needed support from their peers, family members, and
communities, moderators often lack this layer of social structure
and indeed are often unable to discuss the nature of their work

due to nondisclosure agreements, professional isolation, and stigma around the work they do. The relative geographic diffusion and industrial stratification of commercial content moderation work can also make it difficult for workers to find community with one another, outside of their immediate local teams, and no contracting or subcontracting firm is represented in the current makeup of the Technology Coalition, yet legions of commercial content moderation workers are employed through these channels.

In another industry move toward harm reduction in professional moderation work, YouTube CEO Susan Wojcicki announced at the South by Southwest (SXSW) festival in 2018 that her platform's content moderators would be limited to four hours per day of disturbing or potentially harmful material going forward.[15] But without a concomitant reduction in the amount of content YouTube receives—currently some four hundred hours per minute, per day—it was unclear how YouTube would avoid needing to double its workforce of screeners in order to contend with the volume. It was also unclear whether the four-hour figure was arbitrary or based on knowledge about thresholds of what its workers could reasonably bear without suffering burnout or other ill effects of their jobs—and what, if anything, would be done for the workers already exposed to much more than that.

Left to its own devices, it seems unlikely that the social media industry will decide to self-regulate to the benefit of the commercial content moderators it relies on but, until very recently, had not even admitted it employed. Using a variety of distancing tactics, both geographic and organizational, to put space between the platforms and the workers, social media firms have been largely immune to being held responsible for damage that some workers allege was caused by their time spent screening user-generated content. The way responsibility for user-generated content is treated in U.S. law is also a factor with regard to thinking about social media platforms being held to account for the content they circulate and ask their moderators to screen. In the United States, Section 230 of the Communications Decency Act of 1996 is the doctrine that holds social media companies largely immune from liability for material they disseminate on their networks, platforms, properties, and sites.[16] This does not mean that social media platforms do not have a vested interest in controlling the content that appears on their branded sites, apps, and platforms; on the contrary, that desire for control is the reason commercial content moderation exists. But it is largely not a legal standard to which the companies have, until recently, moderated. By many accounts, the immunity provided by Section 230 is what allowed the internet industry to flourish and grow into the economic and social force that it is today. Proponents of this argument contend that it gives social media platforms discretion to allow or disallow such content based on norms that they decided, meaning that they could set the rules for the user uploads they solicited and then distributed. But when Section 230 was enacted, the notion of four hundred hours of video content per minute per day being uploaded to the internet as a whole, much less to just one commercial site, was largely beyond the reach of most people's imagination, if not simply just bandwidth and computational power.

As times and stakes have changed, Section 230 does not seem as unassailable as it has in the past. And as social media firms have taken their business global, they now find themselves responsible to governments and legal regimes not just in the United States but worldwide, many of which are demanding that their jurisdictions and sovereignties be acknowledged and their local laws obeyed. As such, some of the greatest challenges to the primacy of Section 230 and the legal immunity of social media firms for the content they solicit, monetize, and disseminate are coming not from the United States but from the European Union as a whole, as well as some of its individual member states. The recent German "network enforcement law," abbreviated as NetzDG in German, is one of the most stringent examples. It demands that any social media platform with two million users or more operating in Germany must adhere to German law regarding hate speech and content and must remove any questionable content within twenty-four hours of a complaint being made or risk massive fines of up to 50 million euros. In Germany, this restriction is particularly focused on Nazi glorification, imagery, or other similar material, but it also focuses on "hate speech" as constituted under German law more broadly. Love or hate Germany's demand, one thing is clear: social media firms have responded by hiring more commercial content moderators, such as contractors at the Berlin call center Arvato, to bear the burden.[17]

Beyond questions of liability for content, there are questions, too, of other types of legal liability, such as harm to employees. In a landmark case, two Microsoft employees from Washington filed suit in that state's court in December 2016, alleging permanent disability and post-traumatic stress disorder, or PTSD, due to the material—much of it child sexual exploitation content—they were required to view and remove on behalf of the company.[18] Unlike many of the situations described in this book, one factor that makes this case unique is that the two plaintiffs, Henry Soto and Greg Blauert, were full-time direct employees of Microsoft, not contractors, assuredly related to the fact that Microsoft famously lost a lawsuit almost twenty years ago brought by so-called contractors who were, they successfully argued, de facto full-time permanent employ-ees being denied benefits.[19]

Because many employee-employer disputes are now settled out of court through arbitration proceedings that are typically subject to secrecy clauses, it is unknown if other pro-fessional moderators have alleged similar harm and reached a settlement or agreement in their favor. For this reason, this case, which continues to make its way through the Washington state civil court system as of this writing, will be an important one to watch, as precedent is key to successful litigation in the U.S. legal system. As but one interested observer, I have been shocked that Microsoft has not opted to quickly and quietly compensate these workers in order to end the litigation process and the public's ability to follow along. Indeed, other former commer-cial content moderators have followed suit and are pursuing legal means to address what they allege are the harms caused by doing their jobs. The latest instance has been the filing of a lawsuit in California against Facebook by former in-house contractor Selena Scola in September 2018. Unlike the lawsuit against Microsoft, this one has been filed as a class-action suit.[20]

The opportunity for commercial content moderators themselves to organize and advocate for improvements in work-ing conditions has not yet coalesced. The difficulty of such a campaign is, of course, heightened by the global dispersal of the workers and the varied legal, cultural, and socioeconomic norms of their contexts. In the United States, 2018 is not a high point for organized labor across the board, with the ascen-dency of the anti-worker Donald Trump to the presidency and the control of Congress by anti-union Republicans (and not a few hostile Democrats). One cannot also reasonably expect that Facebook, Caleris, Upwork/oDesk, or any other company in-volved in commercial content moderation would willingly ease the way for workers to organize and push back against damaging work conditions and unfair labor arrangements; this, after all, is one of the purposes of outsourcing and using intermediaries to supply the labor pool in the first place, along with taking advantage of the lack of regulation and oversight that these arrangements also offer.

Nevertheless, the rich labor history in the United States and around the globe could certainly inform worker organizing, whether via traditional labor unions or sector-by-sector (as in BPOs), by geography, or by type of work. In the Philippines, the BPO Industry Employees Network, or BIEN Pilipinas, is one such group endeavoring to bring together employees in the BPO sector into an organized, strong community of workers advocating for better conditions and better pay; this advocacy would include the commercial content moderation workers who perform their labor from Manila whom we met earlier. In the United States, newer labor upstarts such as the Tech Workers Coalition are focusing on labor organizing in the tech hotbeds of Seattle and San Francisco, sites where content moderators work as professionals in the social media and tech industries in large numbers.[21] A continued challenge to any organization of commercial content moderators will be in identifying who and where in the world the workers are in the fractured strata of moderation worksites, and if organizers will be able to make their case before the firms employing commercial content moderators do enough to improve the conditions of the job, on the one hand, or move contracts elsewhere in the world to avoid such organizing and demands for worker well-being.

Other types of activism and civil society intervention, too, can play a role in improving the work lives and working conditions for professional moderators. Civil society activists and academics have pushed for transparency in social media user content removal, such as in onlinecensorship.org, a project developed and led by the Electronic Frontier Foundation's Jillian York and academic and advocate Sarah Myers West, designed to give users access to tools to document takedowns of their online content. Myers West published an important study on the outcomes of the project, noting that, in the absence of explanations, users develop folk theories about the reasons behind the takedown of their content.[22] Is this the outcome social media companies were hoping for when they cloistered commercial content moderation workers and practices in the shadows?

Just as civil society advocates, academics, and policy specialists have come together to put pressure on the social media industry to be more transparent about the nature of user content takedowns (most notably via the Santa Clara Principles, drafted at the conference there on content moderation in early 2018), so too could they publicly demand increased transparency for working conditions, rates of pay and benefits, and support offered to the moderators responsible for those takedowns.[23] Inspired by the efforts of workers, advocates, and academics who together have demanded accountability from companies like Amazon and Google and their pursuit of technology development in the service of war or of the police state, a similar movement to bring support and justice to the commercial content moderators of the world would be an obvious next step.[24] I look forward to working with interested parties on just such an endeavor, with the workers themselves, and their needs, at the fore. Ultimately, I am reminded of the words of Rochelle LaPlante, a professional content moderator on Amazon Mechanical Turk and who served as a plenary speaker at "All Things in Moderation" in 2017. When asked by an audience member what was the one thing she would like done to improve her quality of life as a moderator and those of others like her, she said simply, "Pay us." Of course, LaPlante was calling for improved wages for the essential work that she does. But it was clear that her words had a deeper meaning: "Value us. Value the work we do on your behalf. Value our humanity." Without visibility, this will be impossible. And if we wait for the tech and social media industries to take the lead, this visibility may never come. Given the list of problems and criticisms facing the major mainstream platforms and their firms, justice for commercial content moderators may figure low on the list of priorities.

In fact, the creators of the products, platforms, and protocols that are the context for commercial content moderation, and explain its existence, may not be those best equipped to solve the problems it has created for workers and users—the public—alike. And we must not cede our collective imagination to this sector alone. Indeed, there are other vital institutions that have been neglected while the public has sated its desire for information online. I am talking, of course, about libraries. In the course of my work as a university instructor, I have had the pleasure of teaching and learning from students preparing to be librarians and other kinds of information professionals at four universities in the United States and Canada. These are bright, highly educated people with an orientation toward public service and assisting people with their information needs. As the internet has ceded its space to more and more sites of corporatized control and to models of information sharing that are fundamentally driven by a profit motive before all other values, libraries have remained largely more transparent, more open, and more responsible to the public. Media scholar Shannon Mattern has remarked on the untapped potential of librarians and libraries to serve the public in the age of digital information. Says Mattern: "Online and off, we need to create and defend [these] vital spaces of information exchange, and we need to strengthen the local governments and institutions that shape the public use of those spaces. The future of American democracy depends on it. . . . And we cannot depend on tech companies to safeguard those information spaces."[25] Mattern proposes a return to libraries and the visible, tangible human expert intermediaries who work in them to help us navigate the challenging and overwhelming information environment online and off.

Meanwhile, the story of commercial content moderation is being used as a powerful entry point for endeavors that put the nature of the contemporary internet into larger question. One such project, a documentary film called *The Cleaners,* premiered at the Sundance Film Festival in Park City, Utah, in January 2018, directed by Moritz Riesewieck and Hans Block. I served as adviser for the film and participated on panels with the directors. The film covered a good deal of territory I had set out in my research and that is covered in this book as well, including a focus on the work lives of Filipino commercial content moderation workers, but expands outward to question the political impact and social cost the millions of decisions these workers make has in aggregate.

Despite knowing the terrain intimately, I was shocked by the impact the film had on me personally, moving me, in some moments, to tears. It was a good reminder of how important it is to continue to tell the incredibly complicated story of the practices of commercial content moderation and those who undertake it. It was also a reminder to me that our work continues to have an impact, as I watched audiences around the world affected by the film and the stories of the workers it featured. And it was a reminder of the fact that I have an obligation to the workers who have shared their stories with me over the years, and allowed me to piece together the silhouette of commercial content moderation from invisibility, reverse engineering from their own firsthand accounts by corroborating with other sources and uncovering practices otherwise unknown, were it not for their willingness to speak to me. After this book, the research of other academics, the investigative journalism of so many reporters, and artistic interventions like *The Cleaners,* the truth is that we can no longer claim that commercial content moderation is "hidden." But what has to change is the status it is afforded, and the conditions of labor for its workers.

My understanding of what goes on behind the social media screen, in the form of commercial content moderation, has impacted my own engagement with social media and with all the digital platforms that make up my life, in both work and leisure. It is my hope that, in unveiling the presence of these previously unknown intermediaries—whose commercial content moderation work is fundamental and indispensable to their employers but also for all of us as users of the platforms for which they toil—we might ask who else exists behind the scenes of the digital media landscape. I believe firmly that our own understanding of the breadth of human traces in this landscape is woefully limited, and that it therefore must be expanded if we are to truly be able to weigh the impact of our own escapism into digital platforms characterized by their fun, inviting, accessible, and always-on affordances yet that give little honest appraisal of their true costs.

It is considered bad form, generally speaking, to leave readers with a list of rhetorical questions, yet one important outcome for me, as a researcher, is to formulate these questions, such that they may guide my future research and be the many threads that I follow as I trace commercial content moderation

and its workers around the globe, and in and out of the digital
and physical spaces they inhabit. But here is another truth: we
are all implicated—those of us, anyway, who log on to Facebook,
upload to YouTube, comment on a news item, up-vote or down-
vote a post. Our desire—our human desire—to feel engaged
and connected has created the very niche that commercial
content moderation workers fill, the need to which they respond. I often remember Josh Santos, who so acutely diagnosed
the problem of suicidal ideation on MegaTech as one that was
undoubtedly, incurably self-perpetuating. If they build it—the
platforms, those empty vessels ready to fill up and rebrand and
disseminate digitally around the globe—we will come. We will
fill them—with our user-generated content, our preferences,
our behaviors, our demographics, and our desires. We are often
even more directly connected to commercial content moderation than that; after all, it is a user who flags a video that begins
the commercial content moderation cycle of review at
MegaTech. It is a user report on Facebook that sends a post or
an image through the circuits described in Chapter 2. And it is
user-generated content that is the subject of the reviews. Unless
and until we unplug or otherwise force a renegotiation of our
own relationship to the platforms, we, as users, are perhaps the
most vital piece of all in the social media cycle of production
as generators of the content and as its insatiable consumers.
Commercial content moderation workers, who make the platforms bearable, tolerable, and fun, are our unseen partners in
a relationship of symbiosis, the yin to our yang, balancing,
curating, and working on making our online activity feel plea-
surable, like leisure, or like something to which we want to
return. Yet the up-votes, the flagging, the video sharing: our
participation is an illusion of volition in an ever shrinking, ever
compartmentalized series of enclosures, governed by commu-

nity guidelines and Terms of Service, with human interventions hidden away by nondisclosure agreements, and human traces erased as soon as they appear, anomalous errors, in the system. This book, small in the scheme of human things though it is, hopes to bring those human traces to the fore and render them visible, not so far removed from the finger on the book scan.

Is it possible for working conditions to improve for commercial content moderation workers? Until computational power and computer vision make exponential strides, it is a task that, for the foreseeable future, demands human intervention. Even then, human labor, particularly as it follows globalization circuits to sites of large and ever cheaper labor pools, will likely still be preferred. The series of decisions that come into play that a commercial content moderation worker must make about each piece of user-generated content that he or she deals with is sophisticated beyond the scope of any algorithm or filter. The cultural nuances and linguistic specificities only add to the challenge. That unparalleled supercomputer of the human brain, and its massive data banks of cultural knowledge and life experience coupled with its own sophisticated onboard meaning-making software of our minds, will still be preferable to any machine in terms of cost and capability. Social media platforms fueled by user-generated content also do not show any signs of disappearing; the proliferation of mobile computing devices and more people in the world having access to them suggests, indeed, the very opposite. Nor does it seem likely that human nature will change such that the jobs that Josh and Max and Melinda, Sofia and Drake and Rick, and people like them have done will just disappear. And so the need for commercial content moderation will continue. People willing to take on a job that provides little status, is often shrouded by contractual preclusions to even acknowledging its existence, exposes workers to abhorrent and disturbing aspects of humanity, and leads to almost assured burnout will still be needed. I am thankful to all of the commercial content moderation workers for the job they do, as I am grateful that it is not I who have to do it. Out of the shadows, out from behind the screen, and into the light.

Notes

Introduction

1. Other types of moderation, such as forms of self-governance and self-moderation by community members within their own communities, persist today online. Important examples of internet sites reliant on volunteer moderation by other community members include Reddit and moderators of its subforums (known as subreddits), and the editors who monitor and moderate Wikipedia on a volunteer basis. See James Grimmelmann, "The Virtues of Moderation," *Yale Journal of Law and Technology* 17 (2015): 42–109; and Adrienne L. Massanari, *Participatory Culture, Community, and Play: Learning from Reddit,* new ed. (New York: Peter Lang Inc., International Academic, 2015).

2. Mike McDowell, "How a Simple 'Hello' Became the First Message Sent via the Internet," *PBS NewsHour,* February 9, 2015, https://www.pbs.org/newshour/science/internet-got-started-simple-hello.

3. Peter Kollock and Marc Smith, *Communities in Cyberspace* (London: Routledge, 1999); Lori Kendall, *Hanging Out in the Virtual Pub: Masculinities and Relationships Online* (Berkeley: University of California Press, 2002); Kevin Edward Driscoll, "Hobbyist Inter-Networking and the Popular Internet Imaginary: Forgotten Histories of Networked Personal Computing, 1978–1998" (Ph.D. dissertation, University of Southern California, 2014).

4. At the time, many countries were experimenting with their own digital information systems within national borders. The story of the French Minitel videotex system is but one example. See William L. Cats-Baril and Tawfik Jelassi, "The French Videotex System Minitel: A Successful Implementation of a National Information Technology Infrastructure," *MIS Quarterly* 18, no. 1 (1994): 1–20, https://doi.org/Article; Hugh Dauncy, "A Cultural Battle: French Minitel, the Internet, and the Superhighway," *Convergence: The International Journal of Research into New Media Technologies* 3, no. 3 (1997): 72–89; Julien Mailland and Kevin Driscoll, *Minitel: Welcome to the Internet* (Cambridge: MIT Press, 2017).

5. Sarah T. Roberts, "Content Moderation," in *Encyclopedia of Big Data,* ed. Laurie A. Schintler and Connie L. McNeely (Springer International, 2017), 1–4, https://doi.org/10.1007/978-3-319-32001-4_44-1. This encyclopedia entry cites Alexander R. Galloway, *Protocol: How Control Exists After Decentralization* (Cambridge: MIT Press, 2006), and Fred Turner, "Where the Counterculture Met the New Economy: The WELL and the Origins of Virtual Community," *Technology and Culture* 46, no. 3 (2005): 485–512.

6. Northwestern University professor Jennifer S. Light, for example, saw new opportunity for feminist thought and spaces online when she wrote an essay on the topic as a graduate student in 1995, "The Digital Landscape: New Space for Women?" *Gender, Place & Culture* 2(2): 133–46; further, Lynn Cherny and Elizabeth Reba Weise, eds., *Wired Women: Gender and New Realities in Cyberspace* (Seattle: Seal Press, 1996), also held out such hope.

7. Lisa Nakamura, "Race in/for Cyberspace: Identity Tourism and Racial Passing on the Internet," *Works and Days* 13 (1995): 181–93; Jerry Kang, "Cyber-Race," *Harvard Law Review* 113, no. 5 (2000): 1130–1208, https://doi.org/10.2307/1342340; Jessie Daniels, *Cyber Racism: White Supremacy Online and the New Attack on Civil Rights* (Lanham, Md.: Rowman & Littlefield, 2009).

8. Julian Dibbell, *My Tiny Life: Crime and Passion in a Virtual World* (New York: Holt, 1998).

9. Janet Abbate, *Inventing the Internet* (Cambridge: MIT Press, 1999).

10. E. Gabriella Coleman, *Coding Freedom: The Ethics and Aesthetics of Hacking* (Princeton, N.J.: Princeton University Press, 2012).

11. Lawrence Lessig, *Code, and Other Laws of Cyberspace* (New York: Basic, 1999).

12. James Boyle, "The Second Enclosure Movement and the Construction of the Public Domain," *Law and Contemporary Problems* 66, no. 33 (2003): 33–74; James Boyle, *The Public Domain: Enclosing the Commons of the Mind* (New Haven: Yale University Press, 2008).

13. John Perry Barlow, "A Declaration of the Independence of Cyberspace," February 8, 1996, https://projects.eff.org/~barlow/Declaration-Final.html.

14. Jack Goldsmith and Tim Wu, *Who Controls the Internet? Illusions of a Borderless World* (Oxford: Oxford University Press, 2008).

15. Dan Schiller, *Digital Capitalism: Networking the Global Market System* (Cambridge: MIT Press, 1999); Nicole Starosielski, *The Undersea Network* (Durham, N.C.: Duke University Press, 2015).

16. Jessie Daniels, Karen Gregory, and Tressie McMillan Cottom, eds., *Digital Sociologies,* reprint ed. (Bristol: Policy Press, 2016); Danielle Keats Citron, *Hate Crimes in Cyberspace* (Cambridge: Harvard University Press, 2014); Joan Donovan and danah boyd, "The Case for Quarantining Extremist Ideas," *The*

Guardian, June 1, 2018, https://www.theguardian.com/commentisfree/2018/jun/01/extremist-ideas-media-coverage-kkk; Safiya Umoja Noble, *Algorithms of Oppression: How Search Engines Reinforce Racism* (New York: NYU Press, 2018); Sarah Myers West, "Censored, Suspended, Shadowbanned: User Interpretations of Content Moderation on Social Media Platforms," *New Media & Society,* May 8, 2018, https://doi.org/10.1177/1461444818773059; danah boyd, *It's Complicated: The Social Lives of Networked Teens* (New Haven: Yale University Press, 2014); Siva Vaidhyanathan, *Antisocial Media: How Facebook Disconnects Us and Undermines Democracy* (New York: Oxford University Press, 2018); Zeynep Tufekci, *Twitter and Tear Gas: The Power and Fragility of Networked Protest* (New Haven: Yale University Press, 2018); Whitney Phillips, *This Is Why We Can't Have Nice Things: Mapping the Relationship Between Online Trolling and Mainstream Culture* (Cambridge: MIT Press, 2015).

17. Lisa Parks, "Points of Departure: The Culture of U.S. Airport Screening," *Journal of Visual Culture* 6, no. 2 (2007): 183–200 (quote on 187), https://doi.org/10.1177/1470412907078559.

18. Kate Klonick, "The New Governors: The People, Rules, and Processes Governing Online Speech," *Harvard Law Review* 131 (2018): 1598–1670; James Grimmelmann, "The Virtues of Moderation," *Yale Journal of Law and Technology* 17 (2015): 42–109; Tarleton Gillespie, *Custodians of the Internet: Platforms, Content Moderation, and the Hidden Decisions That Shape Social Media* (New Haven: Yale University Press, 2018); Sarah Myers West, "Censored, Suspended, Shadowbanned: User Interpretations of Content Moderation on Social Media Platforms," *New Media & Society,* May 8, 2018, https://doi.org/10.1177/1461444818773059; Nikos Smyrnaios and Emmanuel Marty, "Profession 'nettoyeur du net,'" *Réseaux,* no. 205 (October 10, 2017): 57–90, https://doi.org/10.3917/res.205.0057; Nora A. Draper, "Distributed Intervention: Networked Content Moderation in Anonymous Mobile Spaces," *Feminist Media Studies* 0, no. 0 (April 18, 2018): 1–17, https://doi.org/10.1080/14680777.2018.1458746; Claudia Lo (Claudia Wai Yu), "When All You Have Is a Banhammer: The Social and Communicative Work of Volunteer Moderators" (Thesis, Massachusetts Institute of Technology, 2018), http://dspace.mit.edu/handle/1721.1/117903.

1

Behind the Screen

1. Brad Stone, "Concern for Those Who Screen the Web for Barbarity," *New York Times,* July 18, 2010, http://www.nytimes.com/2010/07/19/technology/19screen.html?_r=1.

2. Stone, "Concern for Those Who Screen the Web."

3. This statistic was, at one time, available at this page: http://www.youtube.com/yt/press/statistics.html; viewed April 20, 2014. It no longer appears to be publicly reported by YouTube at this page or in this way. See also Bree Brouwer, "YouTube Now Gets over 400 Hours of Content Uploaded Every Minute," July 26, 2015, https://www.tubefilter.com/2015/07/26/youtube-400-hours-content-every-minute; Saba Hamedy, "YouTube Just Hit a Huge Milestone," Mashable.com, February 28, 2017, https://mashable.com/2017/02/27/youtube-one-billion-hours-of-video-daily.

4. Cooper Smith, "Facebook 350 Million Photos Each Day," *Business Insider Social Media Insights* (blog), September 18, 2013, https://www.businessinsider.com/facebook-350-million-photos-each-day-2013-9.

5. Nick Dyer-Witheford, *Cyber-Proletariat: Global Labour in the Digital Vortex* (London: Pluto Press, 2015); Jack Linchuan Qiu, *Goodbye iSlave: A Manifesto for Digital Abolition* (Urbana: University of Illinois Press, 2017); Antonio A. Casilli, "Digital Labor Studies Go Global: Toward a Digital Decolonial Turn," *International Journal of Communication* 11 (2017): 3934–54; Miriam Posner, "See No Evil," *Logic,* 2018, https://logicmag.io/04-see-no-evil.

6. Taina Bucher, *If . . . Then: Algorithmic Power and Politics* (New York: Oxford University Press, 2018); Virginia Eubanks, *Automating Inequality: How High-Tech Tools Profile, Police, and Punish the Poor* (New York: St. Martin's, 2018); Meredith Broussard, *Artificial Unintelligence: How Computers Misunderstand the World* (Cambridge: MIT Press, 2018); Safiya Umoja Noble, *Algorithms of Oppression: How Search Engines Reinforce Racism* (New York: NYU Press, 2018).

7. Aad Blok, "Introduction," *International Review of Social History* 48, no. S11 (2003): 5, https://doi.org/10.1017/S002085900300124X.

8. Noble, *Algorithms of Oppression.*

9. Miriam E. Sweeney, "The Ms. Dewey 'Experience': Technoculture, Gender, and Race," in *Digital Sociologies,* ed. Jessie Daniels, Karen Gregory, and Tressie McMillan Cottom, reprint edition (Bristol, U.K.: Policy Press, 2016).

10. Rena Bivens, "The Gender Binary Will Not Be Deprogrammed: Ten Years of Coding Gender on Facebook," *New Media & Society* 19, no. 6 (2017): 880–98, https://doi.org/10.1177/1461444815621527.

11. Andrew Norman Wilson, *Workers Leaving the Googleplex on Vimeo,* 2010, https://vimeo.com/15852288.

12. Kenneth Goldsmith, "The Artful Accidents of Google Books," *New Yorker Blogs* (blog), December 5, 2013, http://www.newyorker.com/online/blogs/books/2013/12/the-art-of-google-book-scan.html.

13. Krissy Wilson, "The Art of Google Books," 2011, http:// theartofgooglebooks.tumblr.com.

14. Alexander Halavais, *Search Engine Society* (Cambridge, Mass.: Polity, 2009).

15. Marie Hicks, *Programmed Inequality: How Britain Discarded Women Technologists and Lost Its Edge in Computing* (Cambridge: MIT Press, 2017).

16. Venus Green, *Race on the Line: Gender, Labor, and Technology in the Bell System, 1880–1980* (Durham, N.C.: Duke University Press, 2001); and Melissa Villa-Nicholas, "Ruptures in Telecommunications: Latina and Latino Information Workers in Southern California," *Aztlan: A Journal of Chicano Studies* 42, no. 1 (2017): 73–97.

17. Lev Manovich, *The Language of New Media* (Cambridge: MIT Press, 2001), 168.

2
Understanding Commercial Content Moderation

1. Kate Crawford and Tarleton Gillespie, "What Is a Flag For? Social Media Reporting Tools and the Vocabulary of Complaint," *New Media & Society* 18, no. 3 (2016): 410–28; Tarleton Gillespie, *Custodians of the Internet: Platforms, Content Moderation, and the Hidden Decisions That Shape Social Media* (New Haven: Yale University Press, 2018).

2. Geoffrey Bowker and Susan Leigh Star, *Sorting Things Out: Classification and Its Consequences* (Cambridge: MIT Press, 1999).

3. Margaret M. Fleck and David A. Forsyth, "Finding Naked People," http://www.cs.hmc.edu/~fleck/naked.html.

4. See David A. Forsyth and Jean Ponce, *Computer Vision: A Modern Approach* (Upper Saddle River, N.J.: Prentice Hall, 2011); Kenton McHenry, "Computer Vision," presentation at the Digital Humanities High-Performance Computing Collaboratory, National Center for Supercomputing Applications, June 10, 2012.

5. Rebecca Hersher, "Laboring in the Shadows to Keep the Web Free of Child Porn," *All Things Considered,* NPR, November 17, 2013, http://www. npr.org/2013/11/17/245829002/laboring-in-the-shadows-to-keep-the-web-free-of-child-porn.

6. See Michael Hardt and Antonio Negri, *Empire* (Cambridge: Harvard University Press, 2000), 108.

7. See M. Rodino-Colocino, "Technomadic Work: From Promotional Vision to WashTech's Opposition," *Work Organisation, Labour and Globalisation* 2, no. 1 (2008): 104–16 (quote on 105).

8. Julia Angwin and Hannes Grassegger, "Facebook's Secret Censorship Rules Protect White Men from Hate Speech but Not Black Children," *ProPublica*, June 28, 2017, https://www.propublica.org/article/facebook-hate-speech-censorship-internal-documents-algorithms; Ariana Tobin, Madeleine Varner, and Julia Angwin, "Facebook's Uneven Enforcement of Hate Speech Rules Allows Vile Posts to Stay Up," *ProPublica*, December 28, 2017, https://www.propublica.org/article/facebook-enforcement-hate-speech-rules-mistakes; Olivia Solon, "Underpaid and Overburdened: The Life of a Facebook Moderator," *The Guardian*, May 25, 2017, http://www.theguardian.com/news/2017/may/25/facebook-moderator-underpaid-overburdened-extreme-content; Davey Alba, "Google Drops Firm Reviewing YouTube Videos," *Wired*, August 4, 2017, https://www.wired.com/story/google-drops-zerochaos-for-youtube-videos/; Jamie Grierson, " 'No Grey Areas': Experts Urge Facebook to Change Moderation Policies," *The Guardian*, May 22, 2017, http://www.theguardian.com/news/2017/may/22/no-grey-areas-experts-urge-facebook-to-change-moderation-policies; Nick Hopkins, "Facebook Moderators: A Quick Guide to Their Job and Its Challenges," *The Guardian*, May 21, 2017, http://www.theguardian.com/news/2017/may/21/facebook-moderators-quick-guide-job-challenges.

9. See M. J. Bidwell and F. Briscoe, "Who Contracts? Determinants of the Decision to Work as an Independent Contractor Among Information Technology Workers," *Academy of Management Journal* 52, no. 6 (2009): 1148–68; A. Hyde, "Employee Organization and Employment Law in the Changing U.S. Labor Market: America Moves Toward Shorter-Time Jobs," WP Centro Studi Di Diritto Del Lavoro Europeo, 2002, http://csdle.lex.unict.it/Archive/WP/WP%20CSDLE%20M%20DAntona/WP%20CSDLE%20M%20DAntona-INT/20120117-060027_hyde_n10-2002intpdf.pdf; Vicki Smith, *Crossing the Great Divide: Worker Risk and Opportunity in the New Economy* (Ithaca, N.Y.: Cornell University Press, 2002).

10. See https://thesocialelement.agency and https://modsquad.com. The firm has operations centers in Sacramento, California; Brooklyn, New York; and Austin, Texas, and has expanded with a U.K.-based presence.

11. See Vikas Bajaj, "Philippines Overtakes India as Hub of Call Centers," *New York Times*, November 25, 2011, http://www.nytimes.com/2011/11/26/business/philippines-overtakes-india-as-hub-of-call-centers.html?_r=1&emc=eta1.

12. See Kiran Mirchandani, *Phone Clones: Authenticity Work in the Transnational Service Economy* (Ithaca, N.Y.: ILR Press, 2012); Enda Brophy, *Language Put to Work: The Making of the Global Call Centre Workforce* (London: Palgrave Macmillan, 2017).

13. See Brett Caraway, "Online Labour Markets: An Inquiry into ODesk Providers," *Work Organisation, Labour and Globalisation* 4, no. 2 (2010): 111–25.

14. Amazon Mechanical Turk, "FAQs Overview," https://www.mturk.com/mturk/help?helpPage=overview#what_is_hit.

15. See Amazon Mechanical Turk, "FAQs Overview."

16. Greig de Peuter, "Creative Economy and Labor Precarity: A Contested Convergence," *Journal of Communication Inquiry* 35, no. 4 (2011): 417–25. https://doi.org/10.1177/0196859911416362.

17. See Jamie Woodcock, *Working the Phones: Control and Resistance in Call Centers,* reprint ed. (London: Pluto Press, 2016); Ayhan Aytes, "Return of the Crowds: Mechanical Turk and Neoliberal States of Exception," in *Digital Labor: The Internet as Playground and Factory,* ed. Trebor Scholz, 79–97 (New York: Routledge, 2012); Panagiotis G. Ipeirotis, "Demographics of Mechanical Turk," 2010, http://papers.ssrn.com/sol3/papers.cfm?abstract_id=1585030; Lilly C. Irani and M. Silberman, "Turkopticon: Interrupting Worker Invisibility in Amazon Mechanical Turk," in *Proceedings of the SIGCHI Conference on Human Factors in Computing Systems* (April 27–May 2, 2013), 611–20; J. Ross, L. Irani, M. Silberman, A. Zaldivar, and B. Tomlinson, "Who Are the Crowdworkers?: Shifting Demographics in Mechanical Turk," in *Proceedings of the 28th International Conference Extended Abstracts on Human Factors in Computing Systems* (April 10–15, 2010), 2863–72. doi: 10.1145/1753846.1753873.

18. Ross et al., "Who Are the Crowdworkers?"

19. See Daniel Bell, *The Coming of Post-Industrial Society: A Venture in Social Forecasting* (New York: Basic, 1973), 9, 13.

20. See Marc Uri Porat, *The Information Economy* (Stanford, Calif.: Program in Information Technology and Telecommunications, Center for Interdisciplinary Research, Stanford University, 1976), 1–2.

21. Vincent Mosco, *The Pay-Per Society: Computers and Communication in the Information Age* (Norwood, N.J.: Ablex, 1989); Herbert I. Schiller, *Who Knows: Information in the Age of the Fortune 500* (Norwood, N.J.: Ablex, 1981).

22. Manuel Castells, *The Rise of the Network Society,* 2nd ed. (Oxford: Blackwell, 2000).

23. See Manuel Castells, "An Introduction to the Information Age," in *Information Society Reader,* ed. Frank Webster, 138–49 (quote on 143) (London: Routledge, 2004).

24. See National Telecommunications and Information Administration, "Falling Through the Net: A Survey of the 'Have Nots' in Rural and Urban America," U.S. Department of Commerce, 1995.

25. See William H. Dutton, "Social Transformation in an Information Society: Rethinking Access to You and the World," UNESCO Publications

for the World Summit on the Information Society, 2004, http://unesdoc. unesco.org/images/0015/001520/152004e.pdf; Eszter Hargittai, "Weaving the Western Web: Explaining Differences in Internet Connectivity Among OECD Countries," *Telecommunications Policy* 23, no. 10–11 (1999): 701–18, https:// doi.org/10.1016/S0308-5961(99)00050-6; Jan van Dijk and Kenneth Hacker, "The Digital Divide as a Complex and Dynamic Phenomenon," *Information Society* 19, no. 4 (2003): 315.

26. See Herbert Schiller, *Information Inequality* (New York: Routledge, 1995); Schiller, *Digital Capitalism*.

27. David Harvey, *A Brief History of Neoliberalism* (Oxford: Oxford University Press, 2005).

28. Frank Pasquale, *The Black Box Society: The Secret Algorithms That Control Money and Information* (Cambridge: Harvard University Press, 2015).

29. Bell, *The Coming of Post-Industrial Society*; Harry Braverman, *Labor and Monopoly Capital: The Degradation of Work in the Twentieth Century* (New York: Monthly Review Press, 1975); Nick Dyer-Witheford, *Cyber-Marx: Cycles and Circuits of Struggle in High Technology Capitalism* (Urbana: University of Illinois Press, 1999); Christian Fuchs, "Class, Knowledge, and New Media," *Media, Culture & Society* 32, no. 1 (2010): 141–50, doi:10.1177/0163443709350375; Christian Fuchs, "Labor in Informational Capitalism and on the Internet," *Information Society* 26, no. 3 (2010): 179–96, doi:10.1080/01972241003712215.

30. Antonio A. Casilli, "Digital Labor Studies Go Global: Toward a Digital Decolonial Turn," *International Journal of Communication* 11 (2017): 3934–54; Lilly Irani, "The Cultural Work of Microwork," *New Media & Society* 17, no. 5 (2015): 720–39. https://doi.org/10.1177/1461444813511926; Nick Srnicek, *Platform Capitalism* (Cambridge, Mass.: Polity, 2016); Niels van Doorn, "Platform Labor: On the Gendered and Racialized Exploitation of Low-Income Service Work in the 'In-Demand' Economy," *Information, Communication & Society* 20, no. 6 (2017): 898–914, https://doi.org/10.1080/1369118X.2017.1294194.

31. See Aneesh Aneesh, *Virtual Migration: The Programming of Globalization* (Durham, N.C.: Duke University Press, 2006), 9.

32. See Tiziana Terranova, "Free Labor: Producing Culture for the Digital Economy," *Social Text* 63, vol. 18, no. 2 (2000): 33–58 (quote on 44).

33. See Mark Andrejevic, "Exploiting YouTube: Contradictions of User-Generated Labor," in *The YouTube Reader,* ed. Pelle Snickars and Patrick Vonderau, 406–23 (Stockholm: National Library of Sweden, 2009); Nick Dyer-Witheford and Greig de Peuter, *Games of Empire: Global Capitalism and Video Games* (Minneapolis: University of Minnesota Press, 2009); Hector Postigo,

"Emerging Sources of Labor on the Internet: The Case of America Online Volunteers," in *Uncovering Labour in Information Revolutions, 1750–2000*, ed. Aad Blok and Greg Downey (Cambridge: Cambridge University Press, 2003), 205–23; Terranova, "Free Labor"; Ergin Bulut, "Playboring in the Tester Pit: The Convergence of Precarity and the Degradation of Fun in Video Game Testing," *Television & New Media* 16, no. 3 (2015): 240–58, https://doi.org/10.1177/1527476414525241.

34. Fuchs, "Class, Knowledge, and New Media," 141.

35. Fuchs, "Class, Knowledge, and New Media," 141.

36. Ursula Huws, "Working at the Interface: Call-Centre Labour in a Global Economy," *Work Organisation, Labour, and Globalisation* 3, no. 1 (2009): 1–8 (quote on 5).

37. Fuchs, "Class, Knowledge, and New Media"; Terranova, "Free Labor"; Huws, "Working at the Interface"; Ursula Holtgrewe, Jessica Longen, Hannelore Mottweiler, and Annika Schönauer, "Global or Embedded Service Work?: The (Limited) Transnationalisation of the Call-Centre Industry," *Work Organisation, Labour, and Globalisation* 3, no. 1 (2009): 9–25.

38. Nick Dyer-Witheford and Greig de Peuter, "Empire@Play: Virtual Games and Global Capitalism," *CTheory,* May 13, 2009, www.ctheory.net/articles.aspx?id=608.

39. Raj Jayadev, "South Asian Workers in Silicon Valley: An Account of Work in the IT Industry," in *Sarai Reader 01: The Public Domain,* ed. Raqs Media Collective and Geert Lovink, 167–70 (quote on 168) (Delhi: The Sarai Collective, 2001).

40. See Brett H. Robinson, "E-Waste: An Assessment of Global Production and Environmental Impacts," *Science of the Total Environment* 408, no. 2 (2009): 183–91; Charles W. Schmidt, "Unfair Trade E-Waste in Africa," *Environmental Health Perspectives* 114, no. 4 (2006): A232–35; Atushi Terazono, Shinsuke Murakami, Naoya Abe, Bulent Inanc, Yuichi Moriguchi, Shin-ichi Sakai, Michikazu Kojima, Aya Yoshida, Jinhui Li, Jianxin Yang, Ming H. Wong, Amit Jain, In-Suk Kim, Genandrialine L. Peralta, Chun-Chao Lin, Thumrongrut Mungcharoen, and Eric Williams, "Current Status and Research on E-Waste Issues in Asia," *Journal of Material Cycles and Waste Management* 8, no. 1 (206): 1–12.

41. Aihwa Ong, *Neoliberalism as Exception: Mutations in Citizenship and Sovereignty* (Durham, N.C.: Duke University Press, 2006); Harvey, *Brief History of Neoliberalism*; Schiller, *Digital Capitalism*.

42. See Jack Linchuan Qiu, *Working-Class Network Society: Communication Technology and the Information Have-Less in Urban China* (Cambridge: MIT Press, 2009), 87.

43. Sareeta Amrute, *Encoding Race, Encoding Class: Indian IT Workers in Berlin* (Durham, N.C.: Duke University Press), 2016.

44. See "Farm Aid: Thirty Years of Action for Family Farmers," *FarmAid. com,* https://www.farmaid.org/issues/industrial-agriculture/farm-aid-thirty-years-of-action-for-family-farmers.

45. Ohringer quoted in Todd Razor, "Caleris Poised for Hiring Spree as It Adds Clients," *Business Record,* January 14, 2011, http://www.businessrecord.com/main.asp?search=1&ArticleID=11846&SectionID=45&SubSectionID=136&S=1.

46. See Bajaj, "Philippines Overtakes India."

47. "Outsourcing & Offshoring to the Philippines," http://www.microsourcing.com.

48. See Castells, "An Introduction to the Information Age," 146.

49. See Adrian Chen, "Inside Facebook's Outsourced Anti-Porn and Gore Brigade, Where 'Camel Toes' Are More Offensive Than 'Crushed Heads,'" *Gawker,* February 17, 2012, http://gawker.com/5885714/inside-facebooks-outsourced-anti+porn-and-gore-brigade-where-camel-toes-are-more-offensive-than-crushed-heads.

50. Sarah T. Roberts, "Digital Detritus: 'Error' and the Logic of Opacity in Social Media Content Moderation," *First Monday* 23, no. 3 (2018), http://firstmonday.org/ojs/index.php/fm/article/view/8283.

51. "Facebook's Bizarre and Secretive 'Graphic Content' Policy Revealed in Leaked Document," *Daily Mail,* February 21, 2012, http://www.dailymail.co.uk/sciencetech/article-2104424/Facebooks-bizarre-secretive-graphic-content-policy-revealed-leaked-document.html?ito=feeds-newsxml.

52. "Abuse Standards 6.1: Operation Manual for Live Content Operators," oDesk, 81863464-oDeskStandards.pdf, n.d., available at http://random.sh.

53. Alexei Oreskovic, "Facebook Reporting Guide Shows How Site Is Policed," *Huffington Post,* June 19, 2012, http://www.huffingtonpost.com/2012/06/20/facebook-reporting-guide_n_1610917.html#s=935139, Figure 2.6.

54. Quentin Hardy, "The Boom in Online Freelance Workers," *New York Times Bits Blog,* June 13, 2012, http://bits.blogs.nytimes.com/2012/06/13/the-boom-in-online-freelance-workers.

55. Qiu, *Working-Class Network Society,* and J. L. Qiu, *Goodbye iSlave: A Manifesto for Digital Abolition* (Urbana: University of Illinois Press, 2017).

56. Terranova, "Free Labor," 33.

57. L. Suchman, *Human-Machine Reconfigurations: Plans and Situated Actions* (Cambridge: Cambridge University Press, 2009); L. Suchman,

"Anthropological Relocations and the Limits of Design," *Annual Review of Anthropology* 40, no. 1 (2001): 1–18.

3
Screening in Silicon Valley

1. All personal names, department titles, and firm names that could identify any of the participants are pseudonyms. My interventions in transcripts are indicated by "STR."

2. Mitali Nitish Thakor, "Algorithmic Detectives Against Child Trafficking: Data, Entrapment, and the New Global Policing Network" (Ph.D. thesis, Massachusetts Institute of Technology, 2016).

3. "Mapping San Francisco's Rent Prices," *Zumper.com,* https://www.zumper.com/blog/2016/03/mapping-san-franciscos-rent-prices-march-2016.

4. Nellie Bowles, "Dorm Living for Professionals Comes to San Francisco," *New York Times,* March 4, 2018, https://www.nytimes.com/2018/03/04/technology/dorm-living-grown-ups-san-francisco.html.

5. Matt Kulka, "I Made 6 Figures at My Facebook Dream Job—But Couldn't Afford Life in the Bay Area," *Vox.com,* September 4, 2016, https://www.vox.com/2016/9/14/12892994/facebook-silicon-valley-expensive.

4
"I Call Myself a Sin-Eater"

1. Names of companies, sites, products, and participants that could be identifiable are given here as pseudonyms.

2. The scholars Winnie Poster and Kiran Mirchandani document the pressure on business process outsourcing workers dispersed throughout the Global South to mimic or take on cultural and linguistic traits of North Americans when serving those customers in phone support work. Kiran Mirchandani, *Phone Clones: Authenticity Work in the Transnational Service Economy* (Ithaca, N.Y.: ILR Press, 2012), and Winifred Poster, "Who's on the Line? Indian Call Center Agents Pose as Americans for U.S.-Outsourced Firms," *Industrial Relations: A Journal of Economy and Society* 46, no. 2 (2017): 271–304.

3. E. Sidney Hartland, "The Sin-Eater," *Folklore* 3, no. 2 (1892): 145–57.

4. Suzanne LaBarre, "Why We're Shutting Off Our Comments," *PopSci.com,* September 24, 2013, http://www.popsci.com/science/article/2013-09/why-were-shutting-our-comments; and "A New Role for Comments on Chronicle.

Com," *Chronicle of Higher Education,* January 3, 2016, https://www.chronicle.com/article/A-New-Role-for-Comments-on/234701.4.

5. Ashley A. Anderson, Dominique Brossard, Dietram A. Scheufele, Michael A. Xenos, and Peter Ladwig, "The 'Nasty Effect': Online Incivility and Risk Perceptions of Emerging Technologies," *Journal of Computer-Mediated Communication* 19, no. 3 (2014): 373–87, https://doi.org/10.1111/jcc4.12009.

5
"Modern Heroes"

1. I am indebted to Andrew Dicks for assistance and insight into this work. As in all other chapters, the names of participants and the names of companies, departments, sites, and products have been given pseudonyms to protect the workers.

2. See Vikas Bajaj, "Philippines Overtakes India as Hub of Call Centers," *New York Times,* November 25, 2011, http://www.nytimes.com/2011/11/26/business/philippines-overtakes-india-as-hub-of-call-centers.html?_r=1&emc=eta1.

3. I do not wish to contribute to exotification of this part of the world: these extremes of poverty and wealth are hardly a situation confined to the so-called Global South; it can be frequently seen in what one scholar-activist described as "the overdeveloped world." Such gross economic disparity can be found in many regions in the West, including in places like Los Angeles, where I live.

4. See Mél Hogan, "Facebook Data Storage Centers as the Archive's Underbelly," *Television & New Media* 16, no. 1 (2015): 3–18, https://doi.org/10.1177/1527476413509415; Lisa Parks and Nicole Starosielski, *Signal Traffic: Critical Studies of Media Infrastructures* (Urbana: University of Illinois Press, 2015); Nicole Starosielski, *The Undersea Network: Sign, Storage, Transmission* (Durham, N.C.: Duke University Press, 2015).

5. See Neferti Xina M. Tadiar, *Fantasy-Production: Sexual Economies and Other Philippine Consequences for the New World Order* (Manila: Ateneo De Manila University Press, 2004).

6. See Parks and Starosielski, *Signal Traffic,* 8.

7. Parks and Starosielski, *Signal Traffic,* 5.

8. Mél Hogan, "Data Flows and Water Woes: The Utah Data Center," *Big Data & Society* 2, no. 2 (2015): 1–12; Mél Hogan and Tamara Shepherd, "Information Ownership and Materiality in an Age of Big Data Surveillance," *Journal of Information Policy* 5 (2015): 6–31.

9. From http://worldpopulationreview.com/world-cities/manila population/ and the Republic of the Philippines, National Nutrition Council,

website at http://www.nnc.gov.ph/index.php/regional-offices/national-capital-region/57-region-ncr-profile/244-ncr-profile.html.

10. See Gavin Shatkin, "The City and the Bottom Line: Urban Megaprojects and the Privatization of Planning in Southeast Asia," *Environment and Planning A: Economy and Space* 40, no. 2 (2008): 383–401 (quote on 384), https://doi.org/10.1068/a38439.

11. World Bank, "East Asia's Changing Landscape: Measuring a Decade of Spatial Growth," 2016, http://www.worldbank.org/content/dam/Worldbank/Publications/Urban%20Development/EAP_Urban_Expansion_Overview_web.pdf.

12. See Shatkin, "The City and the Bottom Line," 384.

13. See Rosario G. Manasan, "Export Processing Zones, Special Economic Zones: Do We Really Need to Have More of Them?" Policy Notes, Philippine Institute for Development Studies, November 2013, p. 1, http://dirp4.pids.gov.ph/webportal/CDN/PUBLICATIONS/pidspn1315.pdf.

14. Lilia B. de Lima, "Update on PEZA Activities and Programs," AmCham Hall, Makati City, July 31, 2008, http://www.investphilippines.info/arangkada/wp-content/uploads/2011/07/PEZA-presentation.pdf.

15. The Special Economic Zone Act of 1995, Republic Act No. 7916, *Official Gazette of the Republic of the Philippines*.

16. Proclamation No. 191, s. 1999, *Official Gazette of the Republic of the Philippines*, n.d.

17. See "Corporate Profile," Megaworld Corporation, https://www.megaworldcorp.com/investors/company/corporate-profile.

18. See Arlene Dávila, *Barrio Dreams: Puerto Ricans, Latinos, and the Neoliberal City* (Berkeley: University of California Press, 2004); James Ferguson, *Global Shadows: Africa in the Neoliberal World Order* (Durham, N.C.: Duke University Press, 2006); David Harvey, *A Brief History of Neoliberalism* (Oxford: Oxford University Press, 2005); Michael Herzfeld, *Evicted from Eternity: The Restructuring of Modern Rome* (Chicago: University of Chicago Press, 2009); Ursula Huws, *Labor in the Global Digital Economy: The Cybertariat Comes of Age* (New York: Monthly Review Press, 2014); Vincent Lyon-Callo, *Inequality, Poverty, and Neoliberal Governance: Activist Ethnography in the Homeless Sheltering Industry* (Toronto: University of Toronto Press, 2008); Tadiar, *Fantasy-Production*.

19. See Parks and Starosielski, *Signal Traffic*, 3.

20. Bonifacio Global City website, http://bgc.com.ph/page/history.

21. See Huws, *Labor in the Global Digital Economy*, 57.

22. Jan M. Padios, *A Nation on the Line: Call Centers as Postcolonial Predicaments in the Philippines* (Durham, N.C.: Duke University Press, 2018).

23. Jan Maghinay Padios, "Listening Between the Lines: Culture, Difference, and Immaterial Labor in the Philippine Call Center Industry" (Ph.D. dissertation, New York University, 2012), 17, 18, http://search.proquest.com.proxy1.lib. uwo.ca/docview/1038821783/abstract/317F9F8317834DA8PQ/1?accountid=15115.

24. Padios, *A Nation on the Line.*

25. For "space of flows," see Manuel Castells, "The Space of Flows," ch. 6 in *The Rise of the Network Society,* 2nd ed., 407–59 (Oxford: Blackwell, 2000).

26. Harvey, *A Brief History of Neoliberalism.*

27. Cecilia Uy-Tioco, "Overseas Filipino Workers and Text Messaging: Reinventing Transnational Mothering," *Continuum* 21, no. 2 (2007): 253–65, https://doi.org/10.1080/10304310701269081.

6
Digital Humanity

1. Sarah T. Roberts, "Social Media's Silent Filter," *The Atlantic,* March 8, 2017, https://www.theatlantic.com/technology/archive/2017/03/commercial-content-moderation/518796.

2. Adrian Chen, "The Laborers Who Keep Dick Pics and Beheadings Out of Your Facebook Feed," *Wired,* October 23, 2014, http://www.wired.com/2014/10/content-moderation.

3. Olivia Solon, "Underpaid and Overburdened: The Life of a Facebook Moderator," *The Guardian,* May 25, 2017, http://www.theguardian.com/news/2017/may/25/facebook-moderator-underpaid-overburdened-extreme-content; Jamie Grierson, " 'No Grey Areas': Experts Urge Facebook to Change Moderation Policies," *The Guardian,* May 22, 2017, http://www.theguardian.com/news/2017/may/22/no-grey-areas-experts-urge-facebook-to-change-moderation-policies; Nick Hopkins, "Facebook Moderators: A Quick Guide to Their Job and Its Challenges," *The Guardian,* May 21, 2017, http://www.theguardian.com/news/2017/may/21/facebook-moderators-quick-guide-job-challenges; Julia Angwin and Hannes Grassegger, "Facebook's Secret Censorship Rules Protect White Men . . .," *ProPublica,* June 28, 2017, https://www.propublica.org/article/facebook-hate-speech-censorship-internal-documents-algorithms; Ariana Tobin, Madeleine Varner, and Julia Angwin, "Facebook's Uneven Enforcement of Hate Speech Rules . . .," *ProPublica,* December 28, 2017, https://www.propublica.org/article/facebook-enforcement-hate-speech-rules-mistakes. Catherine Buni and Soraya Chemaly, "The Secret Rules of the Internet," *The Verge,* April 13, 2016, https://www.theverge.com/2016/4/13/11387934/internet-moderator-history-youtube-facebook-reddit-censorship-free-speech; Till Krause and Hannes Grassegger, "Inside

Facebook," *Süddeutsche Zeitung,* December 15, 2016, http://international.
sueddeutsche.de/post/154513473995/inside-facebook.

4. April Glaser, "Want a Terrible Job? Facebook and Google May Be Hiring,"
Slate, January 18, 2018, https://slate.com/technology/2018/01/facebook-and-
google-are-building-an-army-of-content-moderators-for-2018.html.

5. The website for *All Things in Moderation,* held at UCLA on December
6–7, 2017, includes links to the full schedule, guest posts by participants and
others, and links to videos of some of the plenaries and keynotes. It is accessible at https://atm-ucla2017.net.

6. See the first COMO event's website at http://law.scu.edu/event/content-
moderation-removal-at-scale.

7. Betsy Woodruff, "Exclusive: Facebook Silences Rohingya Reports of
Ethnic Cleansing," *Daily Beast,* September 18, 2017, https://www.thedailybeast.
com/exclusive-rohingya-activists-say-facebook-silences-them; Paul Mozur, "A
Genocide Incited on Facebook, with Posts from Myanmar's Military," *New
York Times,* October 18, 2018, https://www.nytimes.com/2018/10/15/technol-
ogy/myanmar-facebook-genocide.html.

8. Alexis C. Madrigal, "Inside Facebook's Fast-Growing Content-
Moderation Effort," *The Atlantic,* February 7, 2018, https://www.theatlantic.
com/technology/archive/2018/02/what-facebook-told-insiders-about-how-
it-moderates-posts/552632.

9. Hany Farid, "Reining in Online Abuses," *Technology & Innovation* 19,
no. 3 (2018): 593–99, https://doi.org/10.21300/19.3.2018.593.

10. "How CEP's EGLYPH Technology Works," Counter Extremism Project,
December 8, 2016, https://www.counterextremism.com/video/how-ceps-
eglyph-technology-works.

11. Farid, "Reining in Online Abuses."

12. Technology Coalition, "The Technology Coalition—Fighting Child
Sexual Exploitation Online," 2017, http://www.technologycoalition.org.

13. Sarah T. Roberts, "Commercial Content Moderation and Worker
Wellness: Challenges & Opportunities," *Techdirt,* February 8, 2018, https://
www.techdirt.com/articles/20180206/10435939168/commercial-content-
moderation-worker-wellness-challenges-opportunities.shtml.

14. "Employee Resilience Guidebook for Handling Child Sexual Abuse
Images," Technology Coalition, January 2015, http://www.technologycoalition.
org/wp-content/uploads/2015/01/TechnologyCoalitionEmployeeResilience-
GuidebookV2January2015.pdf.

15. Nick Statt, "YouTube Limits Moderators to Viewing Four Hours of
Disturbing Content per Day," *The Verge,* March 13, 2018, https://www.theverge.
com/2018/3/13/17117554/youtube-content-moderators-limit-four-hours-sxsw.

16. "CDA 230: Legislative History," Electronic Frontier Foundation, September 18, 2012, https://www.eff.org/issues/cda230/legislative-history.

17. Ben Knight, "Germany Implements New Internet Hate Speech Crackdown," *DW.COM*, January 1, 2018, http://www.dw.com/en/germany-implements-new-internet-hate-speech-crackdown/a-41991590.

18. Greg Hadley, "Forced to Watch Child Porn for Their Job, Microsoft Employees Developed PTSD, They Say," *McClatchy DC*, January 11, 2017, http://www.mcclatchydc.com/news/nation-world/national/article125953194.html.

19. Steven Greenhouse, "Temp Workers at Microsoft Win Lawsuit," *New York Times*, December 13, 2000, https://www.nytimes.com/2000/12/13/business/technology-temp-workers-at-microsoft-win-lawsuit.html.

20. Timothy B. Lee, "Ex-Facebook Moderator Sues Facebook over Exposure to Disturbing Images," *Ars Technica*, September 26, 2018, https://arstechnica.com/tech-policy/2018/09/ex-facebook-moderator-sues-facebook-over-exposure-to-disturbing-images. The text of the lawsuit as filed is available here: https://www.documentcloud.org/documents/4936519-09-21-18-Scolav-Facebook-Complaint.html.

21. "About BIEN," *BIEN Philippines* (blog), February 5, 2018, http://www.bienphilippines.com/about; and "Tech Workers Coalition," https://techworkerscoalition.org.

22. Sarah Myers West, "Censored, Suspended, Shadowbanned: User Interpretations of Content Moderation on Social Media Platforms," *New Media & Society*, May 8, 2018.

23. "Santa Clara Principles on Transparency and Accountability in Content Moderation," Santa Clara Principles, https://santaclaraprinciples.org/images/scp-og.png.

24. Scott Shane and Daisuke Wakabayashi, " 'The Business of War': Google Employees Protest Work for the Pentagon," *New York Times*, July 30, 2018, https://www.nytimes.com/2018/04/04/technology/google-letter-ceopentagon-project.html; Kate Conger, "Amazon Workers Protest Rekognition Face Recognition Contracts for Police," *Gizmodo* (blog), June 21, 2018, https://gizmodo.com/amazon-workers-demand-jeff-bezos-cancel-face-recognitio-1827037509.

25. Shannon Mattern, "Public In/Formation," *Places Journal*, November 15, 2016, https://doi.org/10.22269/161115.

Acknowledgments

The very last thing to be written for this book is, in many ways, what constitutes its origins. The opportunity to offer my gratitude and thanks to all those who have informed, supported, influenced, and inspired the research and writing of this book, the ideas contained within it, its outcomes, and its future has been such a tall order that I have procrastinated to the point of the editors at Yale University Press moving beyond gentle prodding and, rightly, well into full-on demand. Yet the reason I have found it so difficult is simply because of the weight it carries to articulate my deep thanks for those who have surrounded me, aided this project, believed in, or championed its potential and otherwise made this book possible and that I have had a fear of missing a name, accidentally slighting a contribution, or inadvertently overlooking someone important to me. Please know that any such omission is unintentional, and I value deeply all the relationships and exchanges that have taken place over the past eight and a half years, to be sure, and those well before that have continued to bear fruit in the form of this volume.

Since 2010, I have met and spoken with dozens of people who were currently working as professional moderators or who had done commercial content moderation work in the past.

More recently, I have talked with numerous dedicated people who have been involved more broadly across many other aspects of commercial content moderation, from developing and setting policy for the moderation teams, to working on developing computational methods to assist in doing the work, to pushing and advocating for more transparency and better experiences for people on the user side. Some came from industry, while others were academics, policy advocates, lawyers, or journalists, or had worn multiple hats among these. The conversations I had with so many of them have enriched my understanding of this landscape and have enhanced the contents of this book. I consider them all members of a larger community that will continue to take shape over the coming months and years. While most of those interactions are not captured directly in this book, they have certainly informed it, and have helped me to contextualize the information provided directly by the workers who do appear.

As I set out to find people willing to be a part of the research contained in this book, my primary concern was to maintain anonymity of participants while also staying sensitive and attuned to their well-being. In several cases, the content moderators who spoke to me were in direct violation of nondisclosure agreements, which they were required to sign and to abide by as a condition of their employment. These NDAs precluded them from speaking with any non-designated parties about the details or specifics of their work. Workers were sensitive to the potential for being identified and its ramifications in the form of potential termination of their employment. I sought to protect participant anonymity, while still keeping some general information that would give readers a sense of the nature of the worksite; identifying a site as being a social media firm in Silicon Valley, for example, connotes certain socioeconomic and cultural realities and norms that it was important to include.

Throughout the research process (and continuing through to today) I have operated under an imperative of "do no (further) harm" to these workers, based on their participation in my research. The interview protocol was designed expressly to avoid directly asking about the details of salacious topics or to ask for specifics about the disturbing content they had seen (for example, avoiding asking questions such as, "Tell me about the worst thing you ever came across on the job"). There were two reasons for this. First, print and online journalism outlets were beginning to cover the story from this angle and seemed to be doing an adequate job. While the disturbing nature of the content was certainly an important element of the workers' story, it was but a part of the whole picture. Second, directly asking workers questions of this nature could very easily introduce the potential for further trauma. From an ethical perspective, it was my goal to avoid bringing the workers into contact with further negative experiences as a consequence of taking part in the study.

For the most part, this effort seemed to be successful; in some cases, the nature of the disturbing and traumatic material workers dealt with on the job came out through the course of conversation anyway. In a few other cases, workers expressed relief at being able to discuss their work experiences with someone unconnected to their workplace, but who cared about their welfare, and about raising the profile of content moderators, in general. It is not possible to be certain that no harm was done to the workers in talking about the moderating that they do, but I exercised great care to be respectful and cautious whenever discussing sensitive or upsetting subjects relating to the material the participants see on a daily basis. I have been honored by their willingness to share their insights and experiences with me so candidly and with trust.

To Max, Josh, Caitlyn, Rick, Melinda, Kris, Sofia, Clark, RM, Drake, and John: this book would not have been possible without you. In fact, it would not exist without you. I was honored by your trust, your candor, and your willingness to defy NDAs and other significant concerns to speak with me about your work and your lives. My goal from the start has been to share your knowledge, your insights, and your experiences with a wider audience, and to raise the profile of your work that, by design, has kept you unheralded. I hope you feel that I have done right by all of you, and by your colleagues and loved ones. Your stories and words continue to move me. It is humbling to have the opportunity to share them with others, and to interpret them through the larger lens of the impact of commercial content moderation on society as a whole. You are the starting points and without you this book could not be. Thank you.

Essential to my ability to carry out a creative or intellectual project of significant length is having a close cohort and community surrounding me—a family of friends who have been engaged, formally sometimes, but also and often more importantly, informally, in talking through the issues and ideas in this book, inspiring me with perspectives drawn from their own experiences or points of view, or just generally the kind of exchange that comes from long-standing friendship, dialog, and care for each other. Too often the life of academics can be isolating and solitary; we do so much of our writing work in silence and in quarantine (at least in my case) to the point that stepping away from that work can feel like emerging from a cave or taking a giant breath after coming out of the water. But this has always been balanced for me by the close-knit community of people upon whom I've always been able to rely;

their friendship has sustained me, at times when I've needed it more than I've known.

I include among this group people who are bright stars in their own right, starting with Safiya U. Noble and Ryan Adserias. These two people have been in my life for a decade and over a decade, respectively, which means that they were there at the genesis of my interest in what I came to call commercial content moderation; they have not only seen my thinking on the topic evolve over time but have had a hand in the thinking through of these issues. I love them both tremendously, and look forward to decades more of friendship, laughter, and mutual support. I am biologically an only child, but I consider these people the siblings I never had, and the siblings I would have always chosen and choose again every day. I am grateful every day for them enriching my life, and I thank them for having read versions of this book more times than any of us can count. Traces of their influence on me are everywhere in these pages and in my life. I am the better for it.

Likewise, Michelle Caswell, Mél Hogan, Miriam Sweeney, Molly Niesen, Miriam Posner, Mar Hicks, Stacy Wood, Emily Drabinski, and Mel Villa-Nicholas are wonderful friends who also, not coincidentally, happen to be geniuses. Accomplished, distinguished, and world-changing feminist critical scholars all, their accolades and contributions could fill a book, and quite literally do. I am proud and honored to call them colleagues and friends. They challenge me, inspire me, push me to work, and model an approach to academe that is humane, ethical, supportive, and kind while also being rigorous and groundbreaking. These things are possible all at once. These women demonstrate that fact every day in their meticulous and brilliant critical scholarship, in their mentorship of students, and in their friendships. I have learned so much from each of them, and those connections have been made all the stronger by being able to count their spouses, too, as friends and their beautiful children as beloved young people in my life. Otis Noble III and Nico, Tomer Begaz and Lev, Gui Maia and Finn, Sebastian and Jane, Andy Wallace and Dora, Cesar Oropeza and Xochitl: it has been a delight and a pleasure to be surrounded by such wonderful, caring, and supportive male partners to dynamic and driven women whose work demands and travel schedules could do anyone in, and who have opened their lives to include me in them. Along with your spouses, you are raising the most incredible, inimitable, intelligent, and kind, caring children I have ever known. I have held many of these kids when they were mere days old and have watched them grow up and into their own vibrant, beautiful, and unique selves. They have brought me so much joy and love over the past years, and I consider them central parts of the extended family of friends I have now, across generations. May we give them something to work with as they go on to save the world from those that have come before. I apologize for us and beg of you to do better and love one another and the world more.

So many friends have made their mark along this journey. Ergin Bulut, one of my earliest classmates from graduate school at the University of Illinois, became an early and fast friend whose brilliance, passion, and politics blew me away as soon as we met. He continues to be a part of my life and is a critical communication scholar whose work is political, astute, and challenging to the status quo. He stands up for what is right in some of the most oppressive circumstances facing academics like himself: in Turkey, where he is from, and where he now lives and works. His bravery and commitment to justice inspires me. Colin and Vanessa Rhinesmith (and daughter Lucy) are likewise friends from the U of I who have gone on to do great things in our fields and beyond. I relish our continued connection. Cameron McCarthy and Anghy Valdivia, and their daughter Rhiannon Bettivia and her family, are due special mention for their kindness and hospitality over the years, in addition to support of my work. Thank you to Dan Schiller, a legend of the political economy of communication, for early support and intellectual guidance, and for the convening of the Information in Society fellows at the University of Illinois iSchool, along with Linda Smith and through financial support of the Institute of Museum and Library Services. Lisa Nakamura was an early and fervent proponent of my research interests and supported them in her inaugural research group, where Safiya Noble, Miriam Sweeney, Ruyuta Komaki, and I wrestled with the early iterations of our subsequent work under her guidance and mentorship. This forum was generative, and its impact on me has been lasting. Other important friends from Illinois include but are not limited to Karla Palma, Karla Lucht, Mimi Thi Nguyen, Alicia Kozma, Mel Stanfill, and Sunah Suh, all of whom made survival of a Ph.D. possible and filled with laughter. J. Kēhaulani Kauanui has shared her considerable wisdom with me over the years with great generosity. Valeria Sapiaín and John Beaver and family were important in my life in many ways, and always interested in what I was doing. I am grateful to them for their love and care. Jacqui Shine, an incredible thinker, writer, and intellect, was a friend from the early days of contemplating applying to grad school; indeed, we met on an internet forum for prospective students. Look how far we have come! Molly Wright Steenson and Annette Vee, Liz Ellcessor and Sean Duncan, Alex Hannah, Annie Massa-MacLeod, Erin Madden, Jenny Hoffman, Katie Zaman, "Screamin'" Cynthia Burnson and Shane "Shane Shane" O'Neill, and others are all friends from shared time in Madison when we all were getting our start, or a re-start, as the case may have been. I'm so proud to see where you are in your lives, and proud to say "I knew you when," as well as now.

I have greatly benefited from relationships further afield geographically, many of which began on the internet. Some of them have lasted well over twenty-five years and persist today, more important to me and more long-lived than many so-called "IRL" friendships (of course, we've all met in person and spent time together over the years at this point!). Jason Braddy, Ibidun Fakoya, Amanda Welliver, Kat Hanna, and Ian Goldberg: I'm looking at you. Over twenty-five years, I have met your partners and seen children born and grow up. Rebecca, Miren and David, and Henry and Caroline and Mikel and Loren: my love to all of you. Mis amigas de hace ya unos 25 años y del otro lado del charco: Catalina Uzcanga y Carol Ortiz. Me encanta que sigamos en contacto. To all of you: we are getting long in the tooth, folks. You are the people that remind me of what really matters in the form of your sustained and unconditional friendship. Here's to the next twenty-five!

Speaking of virtual relationships that transcend such easy descriptions, I am so grateful for the support and interest in my work from an ever growing community of scholars whose insights, pointers, commentary, sharp observations, and sharper wit have kept me engaged for years—let's face it, often—but not only—on Twitter, and sometimes at conferences over drinks. This list is far from exhaustive, but I feel I must name David Golumbia, Antonio Casilli, André Brock, David Kaye (from whom I learned the power of a "no manels" rider), Shannon Mattern, Anna Lauren Hoffmann, Halcyon Lawrence, Joan Donovan, Christian Fuchs, Taina Bucher, Frank Pasquale, Tom Mullaney, Lilly Irani, Siva Vaidhyanathan, Jessie Daniels, Rena Bivens, Sarah Banet-Wiser, Andrea Zeffiro, Tamara Shepherd,

Mary Gray, M. E. Luka, Christina Ceisel, Brian Dolber, Tonia Sutherland, Libby Hemphill, Yvette Wohn, and T. L. Taylor. A shout-out to JD Danzler for laughter and love here, too. Biella Coleman has been generous, kind, and supportive in numerous ways; I was so thrilled to finally meet her in person when I was in residence at Western, and so grateful for her counsel since that time. She is the model of a senior academic who lifts up those more junior. I appreciate this and hope to pass it along.

Thank you to the Uncertain Archives Collective at the University of Copenhagen, led and supported by Kristin Veel and Nanna Bonde Thylstrup, Annie Ring, and Daniela Agostinho. They were early supporters of my work and are doing fascinating, boundary-pushing research at the critical juncture of the theoretical and the technological. I look forward to future collaborations. Thank you, too, to Winnie Poster and her work herding all the cats on the Labor Tech reading group, as if being a full-time professor and researcher weren't enough. It's an honor to have been included in this collective. I have also appreciated the progressive members of the SIGCIS computing history group, with whom I have found kinship in interests and outlooks. The work coming from its members (Mar Hicks, Miriam Sweeney, Joy Rankin, Jennifer Light, Ben Peters, Laine Nooney, Janet Abbate, and Andrew Russell, to name but a few) is groundbreaking and much-needed; they have given the world a more honest appraisal of the past so that we may better understand our present and intervene upon the future. Their work is an inspiration to me. Thanks and gratitude also go to the Media, Science, and Technology Special Interest Group of the Society for Cinema and Media Studies. Thank you, too, to colleagues on the board of the IEEE Annals of the History of Computing.

Thank you to all departmental colleagues, past and present. I was offered my first job in Library and Information

Studies at the Faculty of Information and Media Studies (FIMS), University of Western Ontario, and the thoughtfulness, support, and care of several colleagues made the transition into the professoriate, and into a new country, possible for me. These include Nick Dyer-Witheford, Pam McKenzie, Susan Knabe, Paulette Rothbauer, Jacquie Burkell, Marnie Harrington, Carole Farber, Norma Coates, Anabel Quan-Haase, Vicky Rubin, datejie cheko green, Heather Hill, Mandy Grzyb, Alison Hearn, Wendy Pearson, Meredith Levine, Lynne McKechnie, John Reed, Nadine Wathen, Mark Rayner, Matt Stahl, and Kristin Hoffman. I am particularly grateful for the friendship of the wonderful and lovely Matt Ward. I received a lovely welcome visit to my office shortly after my arrival from David Spencer and will never forget it. He passed away in 2016. Thank you, too, to the FIMS students who were so wonderful to teach and so much fun to get to know, especially those who participated in our boardgames class and club. Nearby Ontario friends and colleagues for whom I am grateful include Greig de Peuter and Nicole Cohen, among so many others. Merci pour toutes les conversations à travers les années et pour ton accueil à Ottawa toujours tellement chaleureux, Suzanne St-Pierre. I give you all permission to laugh extensively at my decision to abandon my in-process Canadian residency to return to the United States right before the 2016 presidential election. Whoops. Thank you for your kindness during my years among you.

Since 2016 I have been in residence at UCLA, where I have found support for my work within the Department of Information Studies and at the level of our Graduate School of Education and Information Studies. Colleagues in both the department and the school have been instrumental in supporting my research agenda and adjustment to Los Angeles; I'm grateful to you all. I appreciated the guidance and kindness extended to me by department chair Jonathan Furner, in particular, who has been a staunch believer in and advocate for me since I arrived at UCLA. The colleagues in this department are truly at the top of their game, and their work has worldwide impact; I am honored to work alongside them and aspire to their incredible achievements. Thanks especially to the academic staff professionals in the Information Studies Department and in the School, to our Office of External Relations, UCLA Strategic Communications, to SJ Yoon formerly of the Business and Finance Office and to Helen Magid of UCLA Corporate, Foundation, and Research Relations. To UCLA colleagues Toby Higbie, Ananya Roy, and Laure Murat, thank you for your welcome and your engagement on campus and beyond. I want to express profound gratitude, too, to Dean Marcelo Suárez-Orozco for supporting my vision and research agenda, which included instrumental material support for the "All Things in Moderation" conference, and for advocating for my candidacy as UCLA's Carnegie Fellow junior faculty representative for the 2018 competition. He believes in this work, and his support has allowed me to do mine. Thank you.

Thank you to Yale University Press editor Joseph Calamia, whose calming, generous, and understated wisdom have been present since the forging of our professional relationship. I am so grateful for his vision for this work and his subsequent patience and editorial expertise, which has helped craft a better book for it. I am thankful to Eileen Clancy for her developmental editing of the final draft and her astute comments and additions and for a great sense of humor. Thanks to Joyce Ippolito for her exceptional copy editing and endless patience. Thank you to Ryan Adserias for numerous read-throughs and editorial assistance. Thanks to all those at YUP who had a hand in every part of the development and production of this book, particularly to Sonia Shannon, the artist responsible for the powerful cover graphic. I also acknowledge and am grateful for the early and key contributions to developmental editing done by Linde Brocato. I appreciate the contributions of time and intellectual energy of the anonymous reviewers who evaluated the manuscript at several stages and whose suggestions for improvement made such a difference. Thank you.

This book has been made possible, too, by the financial and material support of the Carnegie Foundation, which inducted me as a fellow in 2018. This two-year fellowship has had direct impact upon the completion of this book and will also help to extend its reach and impact. I am so proud of this recognition and grateful for it, and humbled to be included among the class of peers of such esteem. It was a truly life-changing award, and I hope to do it justice through my work and this book. Likewise, I am grateful to have received the 2018 Electronic Frontier Foundation Barlow Pioneer Award. The Pioneer Awards have typically gone to industry insiders as a lifetime achievement type of recognition; as such, those award winners have traditionally looked very different from someone like me. For that reason alone, I was surprised and honored to be recognized in this way. Thank you for pushing the boundaries of what kind of work should be identified as having impact, to include—if not foreground—work that may be critical of industry, or even of EFF's positions. I display the award with pride, and I thank Jillian York of EFF, in particular, for traveling to meet me in Thessaloniki, Greece, to hand it to me in person at four in the morning as we beamed into the reception in San Francisco. What a story!

To the extended community of current doctoral students, recent Ph.D.s and new professors whom I have had the pleasure to get to know—Sarah Myers-West, Nathalie Maréchal, Kat Lo,

Lindsay Blackwell, Morten Bay, Marika Cifor, Mario Ramirez, Matthew Bui, Britt Paris, Pat Garcia, Frances Corry, Brooklyne Gipson, Sulafa Zidani, Roderic Crooks, Claudia Lo, Yoehan Oh— to my own doctoral students—Ruth Livier, Yvonne Eadon, and Jonathan Calzada, and former advisee Andrew Dicks—to current UCLA doctoral students whom I've had the pleasure to teach and learn with in seminars, including Sakena Alalawi, Gracen Brillmyr, Joyce Gabiola, María Montenegro, Ulysses Pascal, Peter Polack, Carlin Soos, and Lauren Sorensen: you are brilliant, you challenge me, and I see you out there changing the world. I look forward to learning alongside you for years to come. I must also acknowledge the amazing master's students in Information Studies with whom I have worked over the past ten years. As predicted, they are out there changing the practice and the world for the better. I am proud to call you my advisees and so proud of all your incredible achievements. Keep up the good work!

Almost a year ago at this time, a fire raged through the Bel-Air neighborhood, just half a mile from the UCLA campus. It was one contingency for which I admittedly hadn't planned; nevertheless, over a hundred participants turned up and turned out for the "All Things in Moderation" conference held over two days in early December. It was a wonderful and energizing mix of scholars, content moderation workers, activists, industry reps, journalists, students, and policy shop folks. Not only was it the first event of its kind, but it established a loose network of interested participants and parties whose research or work touches on some or several aspects of the substance of this book and beyond. Many who attended have already been named elsewhere in these acknowledgments, but I want to thank all who were there for their agenda-setting participation. Thank you for being there, and thank you so much to everyone who participated in and attended the conference; the participant list reads like a Who's Who of a nascent discipline, thanks to your contributions. I know people are ready for a Round Two, and all I can say is, "I'm working on it." Stay tuned!

A special thanks goes to Roz Bowden and Rochelle LaPlante, two women who spoke publicly and bravely about their experiences past and present as commercial content moderators at ATM 2017. They offered their insights and stories at our closing plenary; thanks to them, the session was powerful, moving, and affirming (the video is available online at atm-2017 .net for those readers who wish to view it). I hope you feel I've done you and your colleagues justice in this book. I look forward to continued opportunities to collaborate to the end of making things better for all.

Moritz Riesewieck and Hans Block are talented visionaries who have become not just colleagues but friends. Their work on *The Cleaners* is incredible; were that we could all hit it out of the ballpark on our first try, as they have with this gorgeous, poignant, and powerful documentary about commercial content moderation and its implications. Whenever they can, they have lifted up my academic work as a source of inspiration to them; likewise, their vision inspires me. Thank you to Gebrüder Beetz and partners for supporting the making of this film, and for including me in your work. Thank you, Hans and Moritz, for your advocacy and passion. I am so proud to be associated with your incredible film.

It is important to me to acknowledge the engagement and contributions of a cadre of journalists and writers who have reached out to me over the years; without them, I would not have been able to share my views with anywhere near as much impact. Their investigative and other reporting has also been key to holding companies to account for commercial content moderation practices and policies and beyond. Thank you to

Catherine Buni and Soraya Chemaly, Adrian Chen, Olivia Solon, Davey Alba, Deepa Seetharaman, David Ingram, Lauren Weber, Louise Matsakis, Jason Koebler, and Alex Cox and all the journalists with whom I have engaged over the years; all are among those whose work is at the root of pressure for greater industry transparency and accountability toward change. We need their work now more than ever.

A note of thanks to the staff of the Starbucks Reserve Los Feliz, where more aspects of this book (including these acknowledgments) have been written than I'd care to admit: greeting me with genuine happiness and encouraging me with pats on the back, supportive shoutouts and cheerleading, and ever flowing caffeine was a game-changer, especially on so many of those days when I just thought I didn't have any more left in me. I told you I would thank you all in this book, and I meant it. The east side screenwriters and I couldn't do it without you.

As these pages draw to a close, I turn my thoughts to the mentors whose guidance, insight, provocations, knowledge, and advice have created a pathway and opened a door for me, again and again. Kristin Eschenfelder, Ethelene Whitmire, and Greg Downey offered enthusiasm and opportunity to me early on at the University of Wisconsin–Madison, hiring me for my first teaching gigs (as a master's student!), encouraging my research interests, and supporting me even after my graduation. Michele Besant and Alan Rubel have also been advocates and boosters. Thank you so much for that. Christine Pawley served as my adviser during my MLIS program, and I admired her intellect and kindness so much. When I first floated the idea of pursuing a Ph.D., it was she whom I approached with what was likely a fairly half-baked notion. To my delight and surprise, she fully supported and encouraged it immediately. Then she threw her head back and laughed when I suggested to her that I may be "too old" to start down such a path (I was in my early thirties at the time). Happily retired from academic life, she is enjoying family and friends on an island off the coast of British Columbia; what a life well earned. Thank you for your lasting contributions to our field, and thank you so much for all you've done for me, personally. I hope you consider the epigraph in this book as an appropriate demonstration of your influence on and impact in my life.

At the University of Illinois iSchool, Associate Dean Linda C. Smith was the one person who was a generous, powerful constant, always in my corner and in the corner of her students. She is a luminary and pathbreaker in her own right, and yet shies away from the spotlight. I want the world to know that she deserves the credit for fostering so many of us through the difficult Ph.D. process with kindness, compassion, and decades of scholarship and mentoring bona fides behind her. She will be retiring at the end of this academic year, and it seems somewhat fitting that this book will step into academe as she is stepping back. I hope she will take all the credit that is her due for my career and my work, and that she will consider this book as a manifestation of her continued support, guidance, and kindness and a testament to her legacy of mentorship and academic inquiry.

To my aunt Rae Ellen Griffith, aunt Kandy Norman, and their families, along with grandmother Sue Kain, I offer my love and gratitude. I appreciate you so much as being constant champions of me throughout my life and work. I love you all. To two beautiful, strong, and intelligent young women, Leslie and Ashely Rodriguez: I am so proud of you and who you have become. In loving memory of Stacey and Sug.

And finally, I close with a dedication. This book is for my parents, Nan Roberts and Rick Smith. They have watched its trajectory unfold, from the very first inklings of me talking about going back to school (and the concomitant and very legitimate parental concern of what that would mean in terms of student loan debt) to this book that has come of those pursuits. Despite their initial worries, they have been supportive all the way. My mother's endless self-sacrifice and selflessness throughout my childhood and young adulthood, to the end of giving me educational and life opportunities, bear fruit every day, and her traces are therefore indelible on every page of this book. Rick's life as a creative artist and filmmaker has also been influential to me, and as I have reflected upon academic life largely being that of a professional writer, I see my work in his lineage and image. I am honored to say that he has become one of my biggest fans and boosters. I love you both so much and dedicate this book to you.

A special note of gratitude—eternal gratitude—to my life partner Patricia Ciccone. A scholar and brilliant theorist in her own right, she has given me strength in so many ways to pursue and complete this work. She has put up with many absences, many struggles, and many endless workdays and nights as I've moved forward toward the finishing of this project. Indeed, I think she could give an overview of the nature and meaning of commercial content moderation as well as anyone, at this point, having overheard me talk about it so much, read what I've written, or been forced to overhear interviews in our little apartment. She left Montreal—by all rights, the greatest city on the planet and who am I to say otherwise?—to come with me to Los Angeles, and it's been the adventure of a lifetime ever since. There is no one I would rather talk to, laugh with, learn from or spend my life with than she. It is fair to say that this book would not exist without her belief in me and I hope she believes it was worth it. I am so proud of her achievements and look forward to them being shared with the world. This book is dedicated to you.

Finally, this book is for Willard E. (1915–2004) and Viola H. M. Roberts (1915–2005). To my grandmother, whose love of learning, reading, and language was her legacy to me. To my grandfather, a World War II veteran who worked in the same factory for forty-five years, fought to organize labor there, gave of himself through public service, always came home at quitting time, and never had to check an email on the weekend. I miss you both every single day.

Index